D1522812

FOR
Tigers Fans
ONLY!

**Wonderful Stories Celebrating the
Incredible Fans of the University of
Missouri Tigers**

By Bill Althaus, Rich Zvosec, and Rich Wolfe

Foreword by Tigers Greats, Players, Coaches, and Fans

ASCEND
BOOKS
www.ascendbooks.com

Requests for permission should be addressed Ascend Books, LLC, Attn: Rights and Permissions Department

10 9 8 7 6 5 4 3 2 1

Printed in the United States of America

ISBN-13: 978-0-9841130-1-9
ISBN-10: 0-9841130-1-0

Library of Congress Cataloging-in-Publications Data Available Upon Request

Editor: Lee Stuart
Design: Randy Lackey, The Covington Group

This book is not an official publication of, nor is it endorsed by, the University of Missouri.

www.ascendbooks.com

FOR Tigers Fans ONLY!

Wonderful Stories Celebrating the Incredible Fans of the University of Missouri Tigers

Special Thanks To:

Table of Contents

Foreword
A Collection of Favorite Memories from Missouri Tigers Fans

We had some great wins over the years and won numerous titles, but two things that I am very proud of are the fact that our players were good kids and most of them were Missouri boys. I always believed that we should build our program with Missouri players. Sure we sprinkled in a few from outside the state, but we gained success by keeping Missouri boys in the program. At last count, I believe there are 14 former players still living in Columbia.

- NORM STEWART
Legendary Missouri basketball coach

Back in 2007, we are playing Kansas at Arrowhead Stadium. We knew before the game that the winner would be ranked as the No. 1 football team in the country. The place was electric with so many Tiger fans that made the trip to be in attendance at this game. As the clock ticked down to the final seconds, I took a look around at the Mizzou fans and spotted an older gentleman in the front row in the end zone. He was screaming with pleasure and crying with jubilation all at the same time. I went over to him and he told me that he had been a fan for over 50 years and never in his lifetime did he think we would repeat the type of success that the football team had in the 1960s. He was overcome by the moment and my wife, who was standing next to me, started to tear up as well.

- MIKE ALDEN
University of Missouri Athletic Director

The term 'Shutdown Corner' originated with Roger Wehrli. There wasn't a better cornerback I played against. He was a great, great defensive back. You had to be aware of him all the time.

- ROGER STAUBACH
Dallas Cowboys Hall of Fame quarterback

I think one reason Coach Stewart was always taking on the media or fans from other teams is because he wanted the attention to be focused on him, rather than a bunch of 18-, 19-, or 20-year-olds. He loved the attention, anyway. He was always the target of the opposing fans; it was never us, it was Coach. He was smart that way. We'd walk out to the court before a game and the first thing you'd hear was the student section yelling, "Sit down, Norm!" He just smiled.

- JON SUNDVOLD
University of Missouri basketball Hall of Famer

I'll never forget standing on the sideline near the goal line of the Colorado-Missouri game when the "fifth down" occurred. The confusion was ridiculous, but many had the same concern leading up to the fifth down – that their mind must be playing tricks on them. All seven officials missed it. I was also asked to go to the officials' locker room and get a statement from them. I truly believe they were just as stunned as anyone else. They were totally professional and cognizant of the magnitude of the situation. As bad as I felt for us in having that game taken away (which would have been a big breakthrough in turning the program around), I felt terrible for those officials. They had to live with all of that. By the way, the (CU) quarterback still hasn't scored.

- JOE CASTIGLIONE
Former University of Missouri Athletic Director

I loved the fans in Columbia, but my favorites were the Antlers. That crazy group was the best at getting under the opponent's skin. And what most people don't know is that they rehearsed and practiced just like they were preparing for a performance. The best show they put on was when they made fun of Billy Tubbs when he got hit by a car while jogging. They had a guy driving a little plastic car and another one playing the part of Tubbs. I always appreciated their support for us.

- DERRICK CHIEVOUS
Former University of Missouri basketball standout

After the game, nothing is better than going into downtown Columbia and sharing the victory with the fans – especially the student body. You get to let them reap the benefits of a hard week of practice and share the moment with you and your teammates. Some guys like to just be by themselves after a game, but I'm the type of guy who wants to share the big-game atmosphere with everyone on campus. I love it here, I feel blessed, and I want everyone to experience that feeling.

- JARON BASTON
University of Missouri senior captain

Dad wanted to wear his MU gear – right down to his Tiger slippers – in his final resting place, so we made sure he had on his MU sports shirt and had all the things he would watch the game with the past few years. It was interesting to watch the reaction of the folks who walked past Dad's casket when they saw him in his MU shirt. They all got a good smile out of it. It was sad occasion, but it was also a happy occasion, because we knew that Dad would be wearing the same gear when he was in heaven cheering for the Tigers.

- TONY WRISINGER
Commenting on his father, Frank's, final request as a lifelong Missouri fan

We don't call him Ray or Mr. Phillips. We just call him Mr. Missouri or Mr. Tiger, because Ray Phillips is the University of Missouri.

- LARRY MOORE
Kansas City anchorman, University of Missouri School of Journalism grad and longtime friend of University of Missouri alum and benefactor Ray Phillips

What every Missouri fan needs...
the Tiger Toilet! Just wait 'til you read the story.

Fight Tiger

Fight, Tiger, fight for Old Mizzou.

Right behind you everyone is with you.

Break the line and follow down the field.

And you'll be, on the top, upon the top!

Fight, Tiger, you will always win.

Proudly keep the colors flying skyward.

In the end you'll win the victory,

So, Tigers, fight for Old Mizzou!

— *University of Missouri Fight Song*

Photo courtesy of Daniel Turner

CHAPTER 1

We Coach the Game

Missouri has been blessed with several great coaches.
Here are the reminiscences of some of the legendary men
who have paced the sidelines.

'Never Fry Bacon Naked'

Norm Stewart is a character.

For years, he was the head basketball coach at the University of Missouri. He won 634 games, was the National Coach of the Year in 1984, and was inducted into the College Basketball Hall of Fame.

"Stormin' Norman" ruled the court when he was Mizzou's head coach, and he stands alongside Don Faurot and Dan Devine as Missouri icons.

Now that he's been away from the sidelines for a decade, Stewart has mellowed a bit. And to this day, he remains baffled by his colorful nickname.

"I don't understand how I got it," Stewart said, arching an eyebrow and pausing for dramatic effect. "I was a docile guy who never – EVER – yelled at a player or an official."

Well, that might have been a bit of a stretch because he did recall one game in which he had a rather animated conversation with a referee.

"We were down by 18 and I happened to call an official over during a timeout," Stewart said. "I asked him if I would be T'd (given a technical foul) for calling him an SOB – a Sweet Old Bill. I was so polite and he said, 'Yeah, Norm, I'd have to T you.'

"Well, then I asked him if I could be kicked out a game for thinking something."

"He said, 'Well, Norm, you can't be T'd or kicked out of a game for just thinking something.' So I told him, 'Well, I think you're an SOB.'"

> **"**Smile at everyone. Your friends will love it, and those people you don't know will wonder what's going on. But most importantly – never fry bacon naked!**"**

"Do you know that SOB T'd me up?"

He might not miss the officials, but the legendary coach misses the interaction with his players.

"A coach is really a teacher," he said. "And I do miss that. But I also miss the chance to be around a group of young guys who are so diverse in their backgrounds."

He recalled a bus trip when the Tigers were waiting for a player who had been on a hunting trip.

"We're all waiting for Greg Church, because we're going to his high school to play an (exhibition) game, which we used to do for our seniors. Well, Greg is late. And when he finally arrives, he has a fully dressed deer carcass in his truck."

The Tiger senior had gutted and dressed the deer in the field and he proudly showed his teammates and Stewart the deer's head, which he was going to take to his parents' house.

"We had three guys on that bus – from New York City, Detroit and Chicago – who had been shot at in their youth, but when they saw Church walk up to the bus with that deer head they ran to the back of the bus and said, 'Coach, keep Church away from us!'"

Stewart still laughs at the thought of those players seeing their first deer carcass.

While Stewart is still a target of young coaches who seek his wisdom, he offers this advice to anyone he meets.

"Smile at everyone," he said. "Your friends will love it, and those people you don't know will wonder what's going on. But most importantly – never fry bacon naked!"

NORM STEWART: PLAYER

Growing up in Shelbyville, Missouri, I was tremendously influenced by my parents, teachers, and coaches. So when it came to making the decision of where to go to college, I followed their advice. I visited Kansas because a family friend suggested I go see Lawrence, and I also visited SMU. However, my high school coach, C.J. Kesler, told me to go to Mizzou after talking with Coach Branch McCracken from Indiana. Coach McCracken told him that if I could play at Indiana, I could play at MU. The more important question was what if I couldn't play?

Well, a couple of years later we traveled over to Bloomington and beat Indiana on my two free throws. After the game, Coach McCracken came up to me and said, "I am the dumbest son of a bitch in here. I should have taken you two years ago when I had the chance."

There are so many people I met when I was in college who influenced me, it is amazing. Coaches like George Edwards and Clay Cooper. Coach Cooper was my freshman coach. He was a three-sport star, an assistant football coach, and a great teacher. One thing that I took with me from Coach Edwards was that if you get too high after a win or too low after a loss you won't coach very long. Another man who I developed a great relationship with was Harry Welsh, who captained the 1930 championship team. These gentlemen were just a few of those who made an impact on me while I was a player at MU.

You always remember the Kansas games, but one other game stands out in particular. We were playing at Arkansas and I was fouled after time expired. I made both free throws and won the game. I had some great teammates like Med Park and Bill Ross. On the baseball side I was lucky enough to be a pitcher on the 1954 National Championship team. Those were fun times.

NORM STEWART: COACH

I was lucky as a coach to start at a very young age. I was only about 25 or 26 when I was working for Coach Spark (Wilbur Stalcup). One of the first years that I worked for him he called me and asked me to go to Kansas City. The Final Four was there and we would be getting together with some coaching legends. In those days we would bring a projector and some game film, so I grabbed the film projector and we headed over to the Muehlbach Hotel. As we checked in, we saw Coach Hank Iba from Oklahoma State University. Coach Iba and Spark were old friends and since I was the youngest coach, it was my job to go out and get some beverages. When Coach Iba told me to go get something to drink, I asked him what he wanted. He told me, "Get one of each and that should cover it." So I did. It was a true educational experience sitting in the hotel room listening to Coach Iba (OSU) and Coach Milliken (Maryland) going back and forth. Each coach would break down a part of the game and then they would go back and forth using their own philosophy to explain and teach it. I mainly just listened. But then Coach Iba looked at me and said, "Norm, you were a player most recently. How would a player think about that?" So I took my turn at the chalkboard talking about how a player might think about rebounding and what technique to use to block out. After about eight or nine hours of talking, watching film, and writing on the board, we went down to the Italian Gardens. Dinner ended and we went back for a few more hours until it was the wee hours of the morning.

I didn't have a room so I just slept on the couch. I had my eyes closed for what felt like a couple of minutes when the phone rang. It was Coach Iba. He said, "Norm, what are you doing?" I told him I was just resting my eyes. He told me you can't learn basketball while you are sleeping. "Order us some breakfast and I will be right up." The coaches reassembled and we went at it again. Coach Iba missed his first two flights. About three o'clock, he picked up his projector, wished us all luck, and headed to catch the last flight of the day. That was great training for a young coach.

Times have really changed at the Final Four Coaches Convention. Now you break off into your own little coaching tree and there isn't as much crossover as there used to be. I think the old way was better.

Another difference is the annual coaches meeting. When I first started at Mizzou the annual meeting would be held at the home of the host coach. It was held each spring in conjunction with the outdoor track championship. The year it was held in Lawrence all the coaches met at (Kansas basketball coach) Ted Owens' home. The dean of the coaches that year was Sox Walseth from Colorado. He ran the meeting and made sure that all the coaches were on the same page. If two coaches had a disagreement about something Sox would be the judge and jury. In the end the decision was final and we all accepted it. It was at these meetings that I developed a great friendship with Joe Cipriano, the Nebraska head coach.

Coach Cip was a very good coach with a tremendous sense of humor. We would compete like crazy, but have fun with it, as well. One year we were playing in the old Big 8 Christmas Tournament semifinals. John Waldorf, the conference supervisor of officials, had come to us and told us he didn't care who was the home team, just as long as we agreed on it. The next day our teams showed up for warm ups. I had my first couple of guys dressed in home white and so did Coach Cip. When Waldorf saw this, he went ballistic. Cip and I staged the argument in front of Waldorf to get him going even more. When we saw him ready to go over the top, we told our guys to take off their warm ups to show that they were going to be visitors and we were the home team. We both had a good laugh at Waldorf's expense.

Playing in Columbia is hell for an opponent. The fans do such a great job of harassing and distracting the opponent. And when we went on the road they could be pretty rough on us. Sometimes I tried to defuse the crowd with surprising tactics. For example, one time when we played at Arkansas I came out during warm ups and went into their student section and gave out candy, ties, and books. Another time we showed up at Nebraska with each player wearing a T-shirt over his jersey congratulating football Coach Tom Osborne on winning the National Championship. Sometimes it worked and sometimes it didn't.

We had some great wins over the years and won numerous titles, but two things that I am very proud of are the fact that our players were good kids and most of them were

Missouri boys. I always believed that we should build our program with Missouri players. Sure, we sprinkled in a few from outside the state, but we gained success by keeping Missouri boys in the program. At last count I believe there are 14 former players still living in Columbia.

> **❝ One time when we played at Arkansas, I came out during warm ups and went into their student section and gave out candy, ties, and books. ❞**

Another tradition that I believed in was not spending any money in the state of Kansas. Consequently, when we played in Lawrence the team either traveled the day of the game or, if it was an early tip off, we traveled the night before to Kansas City. We would stay in a hotel in Kansas City, Missouri, and then with the buses gassed up, we would travel to Lawrence and then leave right after the game. That way we didn't even buy gas in the state of Kansas.

Looking back over the years, I coached a lot of great kids and very unselfish teams. One team that sticks out is the 1993-94 team. They were one of the best at getting the most out of each other as a group. The 1975 team was the school's best chance at a Final Four. There was a play at the end of that game that not only changed history, but changed the rules, as well. With about three minutes to go, we were leading Michigan by four. The winner would advance to the Final Four. Kim Anderson went in for a layup and was undercut. To avoid falling, he instinctively grabbed the rim. One official called a foul on them, but the other official (Hank Nichols) overruled him and called a technical on Anderson for hanging on the rim. They took the basket away and awarded Michigan two free throws and the ball. So instead of being up six and shooting free throws, it was a tie game. After that season they changed the rule to allow the player to protect himself. I would have traded it on that night. Another special game was my first win as a coach at Kansas. We won with no time on the clock by making two free throws.

There are too many players that I have touched and been touched by to name them all. I will just repeat the line from my Hall of Fame induction. "If you see a turtle on top of a fence post, you know he didn't get there by himself."

NORM STEWART: AMBASSADOR

After I retired from coaching, I still represented MU as a goodwill ambassador. I enjoyed traveling to all the alumni outings and golf tournaments in Missouri and around the country. It took me back to my beginnings as a coach when I was trying to promote the program. In those early years we tried a lot of different things to promote the program and get people involved. I started the first radio and TV show for men's basketball as a way to get people excited about Mizzou basketball.

I remember going to Don Faurot, who had become the director of athletics, with the idea of selling season tickets for men's basketball. It had never been done before. Even though he was a little skeptical, he allowed us to do it. Think about it, back in the 1960s, season tickets were $10 apiece. We pushed it and interest started to blossom. Of course, the fact that we were winning games helped a bit.

My role has changed over the years from player to coach to ambassador, but I have always loved being part of the

University of Missouri. Sure, I had some opportunities to leave over the years, but my heart was always in Columbia. It is a special place.

- NORM STEWART

* * *

RANDY DRAPER

University of Missouri Class of 1985, two-year manager and two-year graduate assistant for Norm Stewart

Did you know that Norm Stewart doesn't need to sleep? Well, he didn't need to sleep back when I was his manager and a grad assistant. I was a grad assistant for two years, then went to Madison, Missouri, to coach basketball, and I came back and was a graduate assistant for two more years.

Before I took the positions, all my friends told me about Coach Stewart. They all said, "The man never sleeps." And I believe them. I'm 47 and I still wake up yelling into the phone, "Yes sir?" when I get a call because I thought back then, if I yelled into the phone he wouldn't be able to tell that I had been sleeping. You see, I needed my sleep. Needed it then, and need it even more now. If we were on a long bus trip, everyone would be nodding off, except Coach. If the phone ever rang before 6 a.m., you knew it was Coach. He'd say, "You sleeping?" And I'd yell, "No sir, I wasn't sleeping; no sir, not sleeping, not at all."

My first year as a manager was an experience that I will never forget. He wanted you to be working. If you weren't doing something, you better find a way to look busy, or Coach would find a way to keep you busy. Back then, managers didn't get paid. But Coach believed that if you worked hard, you should be rewarded. So I became his yard guy. Need some mulch? I'd put it down. How about some rocks around that garden? I was the man. And it goes without saying that I'd mow his grass. And I was great at trimming bushes. His wife, Virginia, was the best. She was just a saint. She'd see me out there working and she'd call me into the house and ask if I wanted a soda. No matter what time I'd go in to have a soda, Coach would always come home at that exact time. "Virginia," he'd say, "Randy is on the clock! He doesn't have time for a soda." She'd say, "Oh, Norm, be quiet. The young man is thirsty." They were something else together. When he'd leave, she'd ask, "Do you have enough money for dinner?" She would always defend me and she was always in my corner when it came to Coach.

I never was around a guy who could chew you out up one side, and down the other, then 10 minutes later he'd be asking you to go have lunch. He'd get mad. Oh, he'd get mad. I remember one time when he got mad at me and I was thinking, "How am I going to call my dad and tell him that I just got fired from a job that doesn't pay anything?" Well, I didn't get fired and we all got accustomed to Coach Stewart. He loved us like we were members of his family – his basketball family.

When I was wrapping things up at Missouri and looking for a coaching job, he heard I was applying at Camdenton. He called everyone on the board who was involved with the hiring process and put in a good word for me. You think that didn't make an impact – getting a personal call from Norm Stewart? Guess who got the job?

You could write a book just on all the Norm Stewart stories I could tell you. I remember back when K-State had a pretty good player named Norris Coleman. He'd served some time in the military and he was an older player when he played for the Wildcats. Well, we're at K-State, and I'm walking out onto the court with Coach. He looks over at me and says, "Now, the fans are going to be talking, but I don't want you to say anything." I told him I wouldn't. Coach had talked about Coleman's age, and that didn't sit well with some fans. Sure enough, one of them sees Coach and yells, "Hey Coach, lay off Coleman." Coach just looks at the fan and smiles and says, "Now, I think Norris Coleman is a fine player. But he should be getting Social Security by now, shouldn't he?" I looked at Coach. I had to ask him, "Coach, you said we shouldn't say anything." He said, "No, I said *you* shouldn't say anything."

"I think Norris Coleman is a fine player. But he should be getting Social Security by now, shouldn't he?"

Another time we were playing at UNLV and he didn't want the players to see all the fancy things that Jerry Tarkanian had them do before his team was introduced. There was smoke and flashing lights and they would turn off the lights and follow their players in with a spotlight. Coach took all our guys off the floor and sent them back to the locker room. Then he looked at me and (assistant coach) Bob Sundvold and said, like a little kid, "Want to go down and watch those introductions?" We ran down and watched them, then went back to the locker room like nothing had happened. I still laugh when I think about that.

But I wasn't laughing when I lost his daughter, Laura, at the St. Louis Airport. She'd been in Los Angeles doing some modeling and Coach asked me to go pick her up at the airport. Coach told me where she was going to land, but a couple of the assistants got me aside and said, "Coach might be a little confused about where Laura's plane is landing." So they told me to go to another gate. I get there, and I'm waiting for Laura – where the coaches told me to go – and suddenly, I hear "Randy Draper" over the PA system in the airport. I know that can't be good. Nope, that's not a good sign at all. I go to the spot where Coach told me to go and there's Laura – now, let me repeat myself – *I GO TO THE SPOT COACH TOLD ME TO GO*, and there is his daughter. She had called her dad, asking where I was. Oh, the drive back to Columbia was the longest of my life. I'd lost Coach's little girl. We got back to Hearnes and there is this long walk down to the court. Coach sees me about halfway down and yells, "You should have listened to me!" He wasn't too happy, but later he forgot about it and so did I.

People always ask me what it was like to spend four years with Norm Stewart and I just tell them, "I've never laughed so hard in my life. He was one of a kind."

GARY PINKEL

The Missouri head football coach has won back-to-back Big 12 North Championships and ranks third on Mizzou's all-time coaching wins list with a 59-41 record.

For me, I'm working on game day, so I don't get to see all the pageantry and all the stuff that's going on around town. But I know it's special because people keep telling me about

For generations, Missouri fans have cheered for the black and gold.
Photo courtesy of Daniel Turner

it. We want to make it a special day for everyone. We've had the same goal since we've been here. I think we've re-established the winning tradition at Missouri. We had a great tradition before I got here, but I think it's been re-established. We haven't won a Big 12 championship – which is one of our goals every year – but that hasn't kept the fans from supporting this team. With support, with sold-out stadiums, comes responsibility. The responsibility from my standpoint starts with me, and with our coaches. And it goes right down through to our players. We've set the bar pretty high here and the guys know what to expect. I'm pleased with the work ethic.

I know the players and the fans love the game-day experience. We want to create the perfect environment for our fans. The Tiger Walk, the fans yelling and screaming – it's really an incredible experience for a group of young men who are focused and determined to give our fans plenty to cheer about. As the head coach of this team, I am focused on the everyday things – the process of making this group of players a successful team, a team we all can be proud of. Every day, I want to make sure all our players, all of our staff, everybody is doing all the right things.

I enjoy talking with fans and listening to their concerns and their big concern this year is the loss of Chase Daniel. Any time you lose a quality quarterback like Chase, there is going to be a concern. But I've been doing this a long, long time. I wonder how many fans remember what it was like when we had Brad Smith here. He was a wonderfully gifted young man, and when he left, I'm sure the fans wondered what we were going to do. Well, that's when a kid from Texas named Chase Daniel comes to town and we all know what he did the past two years. He was so good he was among the players nominated for the Heisman Trophy.

Right now, Blaine Gabbert is far and away the best quarterback we have. Any time you have a transition at quarterback, you wonder what's going to happen. I wonder what's going to happen, but I've seen Blaine Gabbert and he is a very impressive young man. We're not going to do the same things with Blaine, this year, that we did with Chase when he was a senior. We'll take a wait-and-see approach and see how he develops and matures into the role.

The one guy we probably can't replace is Jeremy Maclin, who is a No. 1 draft choice in the NFL (going to the Philadelphia Eagles). He was pretty special, but he only played two years here because he was injured one year. Even without Jeremy, we have really good team speed. That's what he brought to every game – the ability to break away for a big play every time he touched the ball.

But Jeremy and Chase aren't the only two guys we lost. We lost 40 seniors the last two years. But the guys who have been here the past three years have won 30 games. That's the reason you look into the stands and see black and gold and not the colors of the opposing teams. You know how I discovered that we had turned the corner and had fans coming to watch the Missouri Tigers, rather than Nebraska or Oklahoma or Texas? When I looked in the stands and they were full of black and gold. People were buying their tickets to see the hometown team. They weren't getting the schedule and saying, "Now, let's see, when does Nebraska come to Faurot Field?" When we drive up to the stadium as a team and see cars parked miles and miles away and smell the cookouts and see that tailgating has become an event – we know we're the team the fans are coming to see. And that makes a huge impact on the team

> What do you call a beautiful woman on the arm of a KU fan?
>
> A tattoo.

– and me! The players understand what's going on. They're a smart group of guys and they know the fans are here for them. Even though the players continue to change, the fans come to see the Missouri Tigers.

That's why we constantly work on leadership skills, especially with our seniors. We work with the younger kids, too. We teach them about leadership and how important it is and how it can impact a game. Look at Sean Weatherspoon. We're doing the Tiger Walk and you hear, "Spoon! Spoon!" That has an effect on players. Not only is he a great leader, he might be the best linebacker in the country. Kurtis Gregory is a leader. He's a high-energy guy who plays offensive guard. And a guy like Jaron Baston feeds off the crowd. He loves to get the crowd going. Those three guys are great, great senior leaders.

We've had so much success the past few years that I don't think the fans care if we are young or inexperienced. They just want us to win, and it's my job and the job of our coaching staff to put this team – whether it is young or a veteran club – in the best position to win a football game. I have responsibilities. Our coaches have responsibilities. And our players have responsibilities. Our fans aren't thinking about things like that on game day. They're here to have a great time, and we want them to have a great time. And the best way to make sure that happens is to win the football game.

And we're going to do everything we can to continue winning and keeping the stands full of black and gold. When you lose guys like Chase Daniel and Chase Coffman and Jeremy Maclin, it offers a challenge. And we love that challenge. That challenge begins when we start recruiting. We're at a point in our program where top players want to come to Missouri and be a part of this team, to be a part of game day.

MIKE ANDERSON

University of Missouri head men's basketball coach

My association with Missouri dates back to my time as a coach at Arkansas. And let me just say that I am happier to be on this side of the Antlers than being the opposition!

During my time at Arkansas, we played Mizzou a number of times. The games were always hard fought and both teams played with a lot of energy and passion. I guess the tone was set by one of the first times we traveled up to play in Columbia.

During that trip, we arrived a day early to practice in the Hearnes Center (a great building for college basketball). This was standard for most trips and usually we could get in and out without much notice from the opposing fans. Not the Mizzou fans! When practice ended, we loaded into our bus and headed for the hotel. As we pulled onto the road we noticed a car coming at us. It was full of college kids. Nothing unusual about that, but then we looked at the hood of the car. On the hood of the car was a bloodied hog's head. Unbelievable. When they saw our bus pulling out, they made a U-turn and followed the bus back to the hotel. The message was clear. They wanted the same thing to happen to our Arkansas Razorback team. It was all in good fun and the Antlers really tried hard to distract the opposing team. Over the years, and now that I am the head coach here, I have always appreciated the support, ingenuity, and creativity of the Antlers and the rest of the student body.

When I was named the head coach, I had a vision and desire to rebuild the program with the same type of passion and enthusiasm that Norm Stewart's teams had. I knew it

> **On the hood of the car was a bloodied hog's head.**

was just a matter of cultivating that energy. The fans were thirsting for it. My teams have always had a couple of distinguishing characteristics. They played hard and they played unselfishly. I guess another way to put it was we were a blue-collar-type team. And that is one thing that the fans appreciate here at Mizzou. They love players and teams that are lunch-pail types. One of our best players this past year exemplified that mentality. DeMare Carroll was one of our hardest workers and helped set the tone that attracted people to the program.

This past season (2008-09), we finished 18-0 at home. Our team was very unselfish and the fans picked up on it. As the season went on, they just got more pumped up and it hit a high note during the Kansas game. Down 16 at the half, I am sure there were many fans who felt we had no chance to win and a couple might even have left. The majority, however, stayed and witnessed one of the greatest comebacks in series history.

At halftime of that game I gave a short, but what proved to be a powerful message. I walked into the locker room and looked around and then asked them one question, "When are you going to play some basketball?" Sometimes all it takes is just one focused thought to bring a team around. Our players had confidence in themselves and each other. All it took was a little nudge to unleash that determination.

When Zaire Taylor hit the game-winner, the place erupted and the place was bedlam. While being interviewed on the court after the game, he just kept answering the reporter, "I can't understand a word you are saying." That is how loud it was in there. What a great feeling.

Getting to the Elite Eight was a great feeling, but I know my work here is not done and I look forward to getting back after it again this year.

JOHN KADLEC

University of Missouri special assistant to the athletic director and color commentator on the Tiger Network

My association with the University of Missouri started in 1948. I had just finished work at the Ice Company in St. Louis and had arrived home at my parents' house. At the kitchen table, talking with my parents, was Coach Houston Beaty from Mizzou. He told them that I could come to Columbia and they would pay my tuition, room and board, and get me a job making 50 cents an hour. My father's response was simply, "When does he report?"

At the time I was not thinking about going back to school. You see, I had spent a semester at St. Louis University and played football there, but did not like school. So I quit and got a job. It was the St. Louis football coach, Duke Dufer, who called Don Faurot and suggested he take a look at me. Faurot's initial response was that he did not like to take transfers, but Dufer convinced him to take a chance on me.

That fall, my father put me on a bus for Columbia and told me he didn't want to see me until Christmas vacation. My parents always knew what was best for me even if I didn't agree with them all the time.

Back in those days, it was a three-and-a-half hour bus ride to Columbia. I think I cried until the bus reached High Hill. Upon reporting, I didn't know if this was for me. By the third day, after meeting a number of students from St. Louis and all over, I knew this was the place for me and I loved it.

Playing football back then was very different from today's game. I was on the freshmen team along with about 140 other guys. They divided the players into five different teams (Black/Gold/Green/Blue/Red). Each team was coached by a graduate assistant – guys who later went on to become doctors and lawyers, not just coaches. The head freshmen coach was John Simmons. He would take one team each week to practice against the varsity. We were practice fodder.

I do remember one practice where the varsity was a little more ornery than usual. They started beating us up pretty good when Coach Simmons blew his whistle. He walked over to Coach Faurot and told him if they didn't clean up their act he was taking his boys off the field. After about a 10-minute break, Coach Simmons brought us back and practice resumed. I always respected him for looking out for us guys.

Did you hear about the power outage at the KU Student Union?

Fifty students were stuck on an escalator for three hours.

Not only was Coach Simmons a tremendous coach, he was a great scout, as well. It was his scouts that helped us beat a mighty SMU team that was led by all-Americas Doak Walker and Kyle Rote. He was also very colorful in his description of the opponent. One instance is when he told us that SMU didn't have linemen. Instead he described them as seven white steers that just keep coming at you. That type of description helped motivate us.

My association with Coach Don Faurot did not end after my playing days were over. In fact, it was just beginning. After graduation, I was interviewing for a high school job when he called and offered me the chance to be the line coach for the freshmen team. I gladly accepted. However, at the end of the season I was told that it was only a seasonal job. I told Coach Chauncey Simpson that I didn't realize that when I took the job, and I probably would not have taken it if I had known it was for only three months. He told me to go see Coach Faurot and explain my situation. So I did.

I went into Coach's office and told him the story and he asked me if I wanted to be a full-time coach. I told him I did. He said OK and made me a full-time coach. A few years later, I moved up to the varsity level.

Having played and coached with both Faurot and Dan Devine, I am asked often about the similarities and differences between them as well as Coach (Gary) Pinkel. I can tell you this: All three men hate to lose more than anything.

Coach Faurot was a very innovative football man. He revolutionized the game with the implementation of the Split T. Also, because he had fewer coaches, we were used to teaching each position. Another characteristic of the man was that there were no jobs too small for him not to lend a hand. I can remember after a big win going back into the locker room and there was Coach Faurot helping the equipment guy pick up towels and clean the room. Another trait that made him a great coach was that nothing seemed to bother him. It could be going very bad, but he still kept his composure. I believe his teams fed off that and that is why they were successful.

He also had a burning desire to teach and coach the game. He was well into his 80s and still coaching the Blue-Grey All-Star game. Listening to guys talk about his preparation for that game was remarkable. He took it as seriously as if it were a bowl game.

Coach Devine was a great motivator. He could get players fired up to believe they could beat anybody, and they did. He would let the coaches do their jobs during the week and then on Thursday he would take over the team and start working on their psyche. As he said, "I want to dial them up one-fourth on Thursday, take it up to one-half on Friday, and three-fourths on Friday night. Then on Saturday, I wanted them ready to go full-out."

In all of the years I coached with him I never heard the same halftime speech twice.

Like Faurot though, he was very detailed. One season we opened at Michigan and they had artificial turf. This meant you wore a different type of shoe. So Coach Devine had me call all the SEC schools since that is what they played on. I did and ordered the type of shoes they suggested. Well, we get up to Ann Arbor for practice the night before the game and we see the Michigan team coming off the field wearing another brand of shoe. Coach Devine takes one look at them and asks me if I had called the staff at Michigan to get their suggestion. I told him I didn't because I thought they might be less than truthful. Coach Devine responded with a look that could kill and said, "Son, we better not be slipping all over the place tomorrow." Whenever he called you son, you knew you were in trouble. I didn't sleep at all that night. The next day we went out and beat Michigan and after the game he came up to me and said, "Aren't we both geniuses for choosing that type of shoe?" All I could do was breathe a sigh of relief.

One game I will never forget is the 1969 win over Kansas. We are beating them pretty bad when Coach Devine signals for the starting quarterback and our outstanding receiver, Mel Grey, to go back in the game. There were only three minutes to go and the game was over on the scoreboard, but Devine wanted more. We threw a screen pass to Grey that went for more than 50 yards. After the game was over, Kansas coach Pepper Rogers came to midfield to shake hands, and gave Coach Devine the peace sign. He said all he got in return was a half peace sign, and that he kept on walking. That was a good decade for Mizzou football when it came to beating Kansas.

During the (Al) Onofrio years, we had some big victories over Alabama, USC, Notre Dame, and Ohio State. The latter were big for a couple of reasons. The win over Notre Dame was the week after we got shellacked by Nebraska. It was great coaching by Onofrio and a little assistance from above.

Following the Nebraska game, Coach Onofrio cancelled the Sunday film session and forbid anyone (players and coaches) to talk about that game. He wanted everyone's focus to be on Notre Dame. He even threatened to fire the coaches if they even mentioned Nebraska. No one gave us a chance at Notre Dame, a team that was nationally ranked.

Our routine on the road was the same no matter where we played. I was in charge of setting up the church services for the team. We would send some to the Ecumenical service and others to the Catholic service. As usual, I would take the last cab so I could pick up any stragglers. As I am about to leave, two guys come down and ask the bell hop where the closest Catholic church is. I tell them that is where I am going and they can ride with me. We all piled in and headed to Mass. At the conclusion, I tell them they can come back with me as well. When we get back to the hotel they try to pay for it, but I won't let them. I say it is on me.

That afternoon at the stadium, as I am standing with the team warming up, I see these two guys come walking in. They were now dressed in officials' uniforms. One was the head linesman and the other was the field judge. I lean over to Coach Vince Tobin and tell him that those were the guys that I had in my cab. The game proceeds, and as fate would have it, there were three or four measuring situations, but instead of measuring it out the head linesman signals first down. We ended up winning the game and I told Vince it was the best $7 I ever spent.

In the Ohio State game, were going against a Buckeye team led by the legendary Woody Hayes. They were killing us in the first half with the "three yards and a cloud of dust offense." Down 21 points at halftime, Coach Onofrio came into the locker room and instructed the defense to play it like a spring football game. We put the linebackers closer to the line and the safeties were only five yards off it. Slowly we battled our way back in. Thank goodness they never threw a pass.

With 15 seconds left, we score to close it to one. I wanted to go for the tie and get out of there, but Coach Onofrio said we were going for two. On the first try we failed, but a flag was thrown, so we got a second opportunity. On the next attempt we converted and won the game. After the game, Coach Hayes was furious. He bypassed the coaches' hand-shake and went straight for the officials. We didn't care because we had won the game.

Later that night back in Columbia, we are celebrating the win at Coach's house when the phone rings. His son answers and tells Coach Onofrio it was Woody Hayes. We all thought it was a joke. When he took the phone, it really was Coach Hayes. He was calling to apologize about not shaking hands. He had watched the game film and the officials got it right. As he said, "You just kicked our butts and deserved to win."

Coach Pinkel has brought the same type of motivation to the sidelines that Coach Devine had. He is one of the most organized coaches I have ever been around. He has found a way to develop toughness without being so physical that players get injured in practice. He is also a great judge of talent and a tremendous recruiter.

His spread offense is a throwback to the wide-open play of the split T developed by Coach Faurot. All in all, he is a combination of both and we are lucky to have him. Mizzou football is in good hands.

I look back on all the years I have been here, and I see all of the great relationships that have been built with players, coaches, and fans alike. As I said earlier, I fell in love with the place after three days and I still have the same feelings.

MIKE ALDEN

University of Missouri Athletic Director

Mike Alden

Photo courtesy of Ray Phillips

For the last 12 years, I have served as the athletic director at Missouri. There are a number of things that have made me feel proud to be a part of Mizzou. There have been so many people who have poured their heart and soul into the Tiger program over the years that I could not do justice by trying to name them all. I know I would forget someone.

At first, I wondered how I could tell how many fans we really had, but that came easier with each year. One way is by trying to count the number of people who are wearing the black and gold in support of the program. However, it has become impossible to count as they just keep coming.

The enthusiasm the fans have for our teams is simply amazing. They have followed us with such pride through the years.

One story exemplifies this. In 2007, we are playing Kansas at Arrowhead Stadium. We knew before the game that the winner would be ranked as the No. 1 football team in the country. The place was electric; so many Tiger fans had made the trip to be in attendance at this game.

As the clock ticked down to the final seconds, I took a look around at the Mizzou fans and spotted an older gentleman in the front row in the end zone. He was screaming with pleasure and crying with jubilation, all at the same time. I went over to him and he told me that he had been a fan for over 50 years and never in his lifetime did he think we would repeat the type of success that the football team had in the 1960s. He was overcome by the moment and my wife, who was standing next to me, started to tear up as well.

Looking back at that moment, I stand in great appreciation and awe for the longevity and depth of the fans that follow us here at Mizzou. That is a big reason it is great to be the director of athletics and a member of the Tiger family.

JOE CASTIGLIONE

University of Oklahoma Athletic Director, former University of Missouri Athletic Director

One of the great joys of my life was getting to know so many exceptional people throughout the Mizzou family. Most of the wonderful stories involve one or a number of them.

Don and Mary Faurot – two of the best people one could ever meet. They did so much for Missouri. I still don't think he receives enough credit for the "genius mind" he had for the game of football and how his Split-T offense revolutionized the sport.

> What's better than a KU fan?
>
> A dead KU fan!

I'll never forget the "Tribute to Don Faurot" we developed in the fall of 1984, the night before we played Notre Dame. The format was along the lines of the old TV show "This is Your Life." We arranged to have all sorts of special people throughout Don's life come back as a surprise. They would be behind a curtain and he would have to try to figure out who they were by the sound of their voice and a few comments/clues to their identity. It was held in Hearnes Fieldhouse in front of about 1,200 -1,500 people. Legendary announcer Keith Jackson was the master of ceremonies and Walter Cronkite had a role doing some special voiceovers including the final line, "And that's the way it was, the life of Don Faurot." All sorts of great former players, dignitaries, and luminaries were on hand. The build-up was huge. It was fun, exciting, motivating...everything one could want. However, Don Faurot, sensing the night may be running a tad long, had something else in mind, when he, the honored guest, is introduced to give some compelling remarks. He approaches the microphone and looks around the audience as to make eye contact with everyone and simply says "Thank you" and sits down. Everyone's thinking, that's it? After all that build-up? People are obviously a bit stunned but start laughing, then clapping, and then give him a rousing standing ovation because they realized Don captured it all with those two powerful words – "Thank You." It was a priceless moment.

Don Faurot was a tough guy

In 1988, Missouri was the host of the Big 8 Conference spring meetings, which were held annually at the Broadmoor Hotel in Colorado Springs, Colorado. As the senior associate athletic director, I was asked by then-athletic director, Dick Tamburo, to go out and handle all of the registration and other administrative duties. All of the conference athletic directors, head football coaches, men's and women's basketball coaches, and faculty athletics representatives were required to attend. The conference also invited bowl representatives and NCAA staff related to the basketball tournament. Don Faurot, roughly 86 years old at the time, was still one of the main guys behind the College All-Star game, which was called the Blue-Gray Classic. So he's in attendance and happened to be in the registration room at the time Billy Tubbs (the Oklahoma basketball coach) and his wife walked in. Coach Faurot gets up out of his seat to greet them and somehow stumbles over one of the ottomans in front of a chair. He takes a very hard fall. We get an ambulance (against his wishes) and we're going to take him to the hospital to have him examined. We think he's hurt more than he is letting on. I accompany him to the hospital and we're there about four hours. Of course, he doesn't like all the fuss and tries to get me to take him back to the hotel. We wait until the doctor finishes his work and releases him. The final diagnosis – a fractured pelvis. He prescribed strict bed rest. Obviously, he's sore but can walk gingerly. I get him back to his room and arrange for some items he needed and we plan to constantly check on him.

That evening, we go up to the room to check on him and he's not there. Somehow he got himself dressed and came down to the opening dinner and was sitting in a chair (on a small pillow) there in the ballroom, but obviously in some pain. I said, "Coach, you don't need to be here." But he insisted that he came all the way out there and wasn't going to miss it. The next day we arranged for a plane to take him back to Columbia where he was supposed to be confined for seven days of bed rest. When I returned to Columbia, I was told he was spotted driving his car a couple days after he was home. Once he got something in his mind, he wasn't going to be denied.

It gave special meaning to the phrase he always used when talking about his positive approach to living his life.

Other Memories

I'll never forget standing on the sideline near the goal line of the Colorado-Missouri game when the fifth down occurred. The confusion was ridiculous, but many had the same concern leading up to the fifth down – that their mind must be playing tricks on them. All seven officials missed it. I was also asked to go to the officials' locker room and get a statement from them. I truly believe they were just as stunned as anyone else. They were totally professional and cognizant of the magnitude of the situation. As bad as I felt for us in having that game taken away (which would have been a big breakthrough in turning the program around), I felt terrible for those officials. They had to live with all of that. By the way, the Colorado quarterback still hasn't scored.

> **" By the way, the Colorado quarterback still hasn't scored. "**

Great moments I'll never forget

Triple overtime win over Illinois in the St. Louis Arena

It took some Illinois' missed free throws to "open the door," but Norm Stewart was absolutely masterful (as usual) in putting his team in position to win. A number of Tiger players had already fouled out, but our players were tenacious and really played one of the greatest games ever.

1997 The Immaculate Deflection:

The setting on a fall Missouri afternoon was perfect. No. 1 Nebraska visits Faurot Field and, for the first time in 20 years, the stadium was full of Tiger fans – not the traveling "sea of red." The largest crowd since the early 1980s saw a tremendous game only to end in the most unexpected and gut-wrenching way. In spite of it all, Missouri football proved it was finally coming back.

Traveling to almost every Missouri town with "Mr. Mizzou," Jon Kadlec. Before Mapquest or Google maps, John had a route to every town based on the local restaurants and/or the local Dairy Queen. Talk about a beloved figure in Missouri history, John Kadlec is the best.

Great people

Norm Stewart ... the best competitor I've ever met or watched. Simply extraordinary what he achieved as a player and coach.

Bob Broeg ... (former sports director of *St. Louis Post-Dispatch*) exceptional writer and historian of our time.

Dave Hart ... (former athletic director) accomplished a lot for Missouri but was often misunderstood. Very underappreciated.

Dr. Chuck Keisler ... (former Chancellor of Missouri) was one of the most influential figures in helping integrate the athletics program with the academic mission. He deserves a lot of credit for helping provide critical leadership which led to the renaissance in Missouri football and the rest of the athletic program. He supported the Master

Facilities Plan to construct "The Sports Park at MU." He was a terrific leader throughout the entire campus.

Dan Devine ... extraordinary coach and master motivator. He had a magical gift to inspire people.

CHAPTER 2

We Play the Game

College athletics are really all about the players ... the student-athletes who give their hearts and souls to their teams.

In this chapter, some of Mizzou's all-time great players recall their favorite memories.

STEVE STIPANOVICH

University of Missouri Class of 1983, who teamed with Jon Sundvold to lead the Tigers to four consecutive Big 8 championships

Coming out of DeSmet High School, I visited UCLA, North Carolina, Notre Dame, Kentucky, Duke, and Missouri. The other schools had more national reputations, but something drew me to Missouri. I had met John Sundvold a few times during our high school careers and knew that if I went to Mizzou that we would have an opportunity to play together. Also, there was something that was cool about playing in your home state. And finally, they did a great job of recruiting me.

During my senior year we played at Jefferson City High School. Coach (Norm) Stewart led a contingent of fans over to Jeff City that night that was unbelievable. There were so many Mizzou fans cheering for us that I think I scored 45 points that night. The number of signs that the fans brought with them urging me to come to Mizzou was astounding. They even had banners and buttons made up. That really sold me on going to MU.

My four years there were unbelievable. We were fortunate enough to win over 100 games and four Big 8 titles. Playing in front of packed houses at Hearnes Arena was a great feeling. The Antlers were in rare form most nights. They were the best fans at being creative without throwing things at the opponent. If you had a flaw in your game or your body, they jumped on it. Now, when you went to opposing arenas their fans could be just as nasty, but they usually resorted to throwing objects at you. Over the years

"Sometimes the fans even spit on you. We took that as a badge of honor."

we went into places and brought out some of the nastiness in fans. (I guess it was because we were on top at that point.) Some nights it was popcorns and hot dogs. Other nights it was bottles and cans. Sometimes they even spit on you. We took that as a badge of honor. The final thought about the fans was that they were always there to support us. Not only did they come to games, but when we played on the road there were always a lot of fans waiting at the airport to greet our plane when we landed. That was a truly great feeling.

Starting on the first day, you were indoctrinated into hating Kansas. Coach Stewart never took us to stay in Kansas. We didn't even eat any meals in the state; that's how strongly he felt. The other thing you could on count on with Coach Stewart was that his teams were going to play man-to-man defense. He said many times that teams that played zone just didn't want to play defense. In my four years, you could count on one hand how many games we played zone defense.

One time that we did, it won us a game. Late in the season we were preparing for a game against Kansas State and one practice Coach put in a zone defense. We practiced it, but never thought we would ever play it in a game. That was against his philosophy. Well, we get late in the game against Kansas State and he calls time out. He instructs us to switch to the zone defense we had been working on. It totally threw them off and we ended up winning the game.

I am proud of the fact that I was on a team that was good enough to be ranked No. 1 in the country. And in my senior year we beat a very good University of North Carolina team that was loaded with players from all over the country. As the game wound down I looked around and saw something amazing. All five players on the floor for Missouri were from the state. Playing with Jon Sundvold was a great feeling. He was one of the best athletes I ever played with. There was nothing he couldn't do. It was fun being the inside punch to his outside game. One thing Coach always wanted to do was win with Missouri guys. We were his proof that it could be done with in-state players.

Now life has come full circle. My daughter is a junior at Mizzou. Also, I have been asked to be the Grand Marshall, along with Jon Sundvold, at this year's Homecoming festivities.

KIM ANDERSON

Big 8 Player of the Year in 1977

I was part of the Missouri basketball program for 15 years. My first four were as a player. I then served as an assistant on two different occasions for a total of eleven years. My association with Mizzou has been one of the great experiences of my life. I was lucky enough to witness the program from the perspective of a student-athlete and a coach under Norm Stewart. It was a tremendous learning experience.

Playing for Coach Stewart taught you to play all-out at all times. It was a physical style that we had in those days. I guess I took that message to heart because I own the school record for disqualifications from a game. I fouled out 36 times over my four-year career, which included 13 in one season. He taught me to be a fighter in the positive sense. He was a great motivator and helped prepare us to the point where it didn't matter if we were up 10 or down 10, we were going to play with the same intensity and intelligence level.

You had to bring the same energy to practice or you would find yourself on the bench. My first day of practice, I showed up and there were 27 other guys on scholarship. Back then, we still had a junior varsity team and he would use that team to teach you a lesson. I remember during my freshman season, I came back late in the year from an injury and started three games in a row. I thought I had arrived, but Coach thought otherwise. I had started a game on Saturday against Oklahoma and had not performed as well as he thought I should have, so he called me on Sunday and told me that I would be suiting up for the junior varsity game on Monday against Central Methodist JV. I didn't quite understand it. To rub salt in the wound, I didn't even start the JV game. How about that? I am playing against mighty Oklahoma on Saturday and then not even starting a JV game two days later. When I asked him later why he did that, he said, "What does it matter who you play against? You should just play." After I graduated I came to appreciate his ability to see the big picture.

> How can you tell if a K-Stater is a married man?
>
> There's tobacco juice running down both doors of his pickup.

One thing about Coach Stewart is that he wanted to win at everything. It didn't matter if it was playing cards on the plane or out on the golf course. You'd better bring your best because he was. One time I was paired with Coach in a foursome. We lost and the pair we were playing agreed to play again in the future. That wasn't good enough for Coach; he wanted to play again the next morning.

In 1976 we were going for Coach's first Big 8 title and we were playing at Kansas State for a chance to clinch a tie for the regular season crown. Coach always looked for an emotional edge against another team and its coach. In this case it was Jack Hartman. Well, we're sitting in the locker room and Coach sends the manager out to see if Kansas State had taken the floor yet. When the manager came back and said they had not, Coach decided that we would not be the first team out on the floor. So we are sitting in the locker room as the clock is running down. At the 10-minute mark he sent the manager out again. He came back with the same answer. Still no Kansas State. Finally, with about seven minutes left, the manager notified Coach that they had taken the floor. At that point he pulled us together and sent us out on the floor. In his mind he had already beaten Coach Hartman. And just as he had won the coach's duel, we went out and beat the Wildcats to clinch the first Big 8 title in Coach Stewart's career. It was the first of many to come.

Playing in Hearnes was a fantastic home court advantage. The Antlers made sure that they did their best to distract and provoke the opponent. It started long before game time. The night before the game, they would choose a player from the visiting team and have pizzas delivered to him all night long. One such player was Dean Yudoff from Iowa State. He was one of their better post players. However, after a night of pizza delivery, he played like he had lead in his feet.

Another trick the Antlers pulled was to time it just right when the opponent's bus was leaving the hotel. Most teams stayed at the Holiday Inn on Stadium Boulevard. Back then, it was a two-lane road to the arena. Once they were in front of the bus they would slow down to a crawl and back up traffic for a couple of miles. A drive that would normally take 10 minutes would take the visiting team about 30 minutes. They probably could have walked to the arena faster.

Working for Coach Stewart was a treat on numerous levels. He taught you so much about the game. He was great at the big picture. He could see things in a game that had not happened yet. He always seemed to be one step ahead. Traveling the back roads of Missouri recruiting with Coach was also an adventure. Upon leaving school we would always stop at the convenience store where he would pick up a cola and a bag of peanuts. Not that unusual, but when he dumped the bag of peanuts into the cola, I was stunned. For years we would travel together and the ritual would be the same. After dumping the bag of peanuts into the cola, he would proceed to eat them like most people would eat popcorn.

As a coach, you could not ask for a better teacher than Coach Stewart. As a player from Missouri, it was a special honor to play at the university.

JIM WHITE

Former Missouri football player

I was a football player at Truman High School when some of my teammates and I went to see the University of Nebraska at Missouri game. As the bus turned down Stadium

Boulevard, I saw the Tiger paws on the road leading to the stadium and thought that it was one of the coolest things I had ever seen. As I watched Coach Woody Widenhofer prowl the sidelines, I saw myself in a Tiger uniform. As we rode back on the bus that day I told my twin brother (Tom) that it would be a dream-come-true if we could play football at the University of Missouri.

> **"I figured I was going to be No.10, but then they duct-taped a 7 on the jersey and I became No. 107. That's how far down on the depth chart I was that first day."**

I had an opportunity to go play football at a number of different colleges, but I had my heart set on playing at Mizzou. With the help of my high school coach, Dave McGraw, I got invited to walk-on tryouts. That was the first step. When I showed up for the first day there were over 100 guys all trying to make the team. I figured I was going to be No. 10, but then they duct-taped a 7 on the jersey and I became No. 107. That's how far down on the depth chart I was that first day.

Practice started and I was trying to do anything that would make me stand out. Being a member of the scout team, you wanted to do something to show the coaches you could play, but at the same time, the starters didn't want you to go full-out and risk injury. Competing against scholarship athletes, it was a question of paying our dues. And I loved every minute of it, especially that I was able to live out my dream with Tom doing it, as well. But I wanted to do more. This wasn't the easiest thing to do since most of the other players were bigger, faster, and stronger. Tony Van Zandt was a Parade All-America, and Darrell Wallace was nearing the rushing record, so my future as a running back didn't look very bright. Thanks to a major flood in 1986 that knocked out part of I-70, I got my chance.

My parents always taught me to call if you were going to be late. So I called the coaches, and even though I am not sure they even knew who we were, it paid off. As it turned out we weren't the only ones late for practice, but not many players called. The coaches were upset and they rewarded those players that called. I went from the back of the line to starting a junior varsity game vs. William Jewel. As fate would have it, Coach Widenhofer came to the game and I had about 180 all-purpose yards. After that game he knew who I was and I got a chance to play in all of the junior varsity games.

I always believed since Coach Woody was from Pittsburgh he would like hard-nosed players like my brother and me. Even though I didn't have the build of a Division I player, I was his type of blue-collar player. After my freshman year, they did away with the junior varsity team so it was back to the scout team for my sophomore year.

In the spring going into my junior year, I caught another break when a new running back coach was hired. Coach Frank Novak came in and changed my life. I was last string for the previous coach. However, when Coach Novak came in, he evaluated each of us from Day One and never looked at anything in the previous year's performance. After my first week of practice I was elevated to first string. Everyone, including me, was in shock. From that point on I gained tremendous confidence and knew I needed to be on the top of my game.

My first game was against Utah State. I can remember standing on the sideline thinking, wow, three years ago this was just a dream. My biggest moments were when I called my father to tell him I was the starting running back at Missouri and scoring the winning touchdown against TCU. Also, when both Tom and I got to play in the Kansas State game. (Jim's twin brother, Tom, earned three letters in track and two in football.)

JOHNNY ROLAND

University of Missouri running back great

Growing up in Texas back in the early 1960s, you knew you were going to a school out of state if you wanted to play at the highest level. Back then the Southwest Conference did not recruit minority players. Their loss was Missouri's gain. When I was coming out of high school, the rule was that you couldn't visit a college until after your spring season was done. Since I played baseball, it wasn't until after the season that I made my college visits to Indiana, Oklahoma, and Missouri.

At first, I committed to Oklahoma, but after I visited Missouri I changed my mind. A couple of things factored into my decision. First, the people I met in Columbia were good people. Guys like Norris Stephenson and Mel West were still around the program (always a good sign when former players still want to be around the program). Some of the other players that stuck out were guys like George Seals, Bill Tobin, and Andy Russell. Overall, there was just such a good

Did you hear about the new $3 million Kansas lottery?

The winner gets 3 dollars per year for a million years.

feeling on campus. As it turned out, I was the first major recruit outside of the state of Missouri. The second factor was that Columbia was close to two major cities. I figured if football didn't work out for me that I could always get a job in Kansas City or St. Louis. As it turned out, football worked out very well.

Playing for Coach (Dan) Devine, you always knew what was expected. There was nothing fancy to his strategy. We were going to play power football. On offense we were going to run the ball and execute. "Power sweep left" and "power sweep right" were our two favorite plays. It was like the motto that Colonel Sanders (of Kentucky Fried Chicken) had for his business. "Do one thing and do it well."

There were not a lot of games that stick out in my mind, but two that do were my first and last games. In my first game as a sophomore (freshmen weren't eligible in those days), we played the University of California. They had a quarterback by the name of Craig Morton who went on to play in the NFL. He could really throw the ball so our strategy was simple. Keep the ball away from their offense. That day we did a great job of controlling the football. By the end of the game I had scored three touchdowns and we had won easily.

Coach Devine didn't stray from his game plan no matter what other teams did. Sometimes coaches over-thought the game and tricked themselves out. For example, in 1964 we were playing a good Kansas team led by Gale Sayers. Their coach thought that if he spread Sayers out he could get him the ball in the open field. However, we put so much pressure on the quarterback that he didn't have time to get the ball to

Sayers. With him neutralized, the game was not that hard to win.

Playing against your archrivals is special. At Missouri, coaches and players are judged by if they beat Kansas. Needless to say, your season wasn't considered a success unless you beat them. I am proud to say that I never lost to the hated Jayhawks. In fact, my last game was against Kansas and I scored three touchdowns. Now that was a good feeling!

I always tried to be a student of the game and after graduation it paid off. When my playing days were over, Coach Devine hired me on his staff at Notre Dame. I will always be appreciative for that.

Looking back on my time at Mizzou, I really grew to love the people and the state. And many of the players mentioned above have become life-long friends. Playing in what has become the glory days of Mizzou football was as good as it gets. Now I go back and watch Coach (Gary) Pinkel build the same type of program.

> Did you hear about the Oklahoma linebacker who stole a police car?
>
> He saw "911" on the side and thought it was a Porsche.

ROGER STAUBACH

Hall of Fame quarterback of the Dallas Cowboys

"The term 'Shutdown Corner' originated with Roger Wehrli. There wasn't a better cornerback I played against. He was a great, great defensive back. You had to be aware of him all the time."

ROGER WEHRLI

A two-time All-Big 8 player, Wehrli was the Big 8 Defensive Player of the Year as a senior. That same year, he was also a unanimous All-America selection.

I believe the same sign leads into King City (Missouri) that was there back when I was in high school: KING CITY, Population 1,003. There were 28 students in my graduating class and I wound up playing at the University of Missouri, then for the hometown NFL team – the St. Louis Cardinals – and I also wound up in a few halls of fame. Talk about a dream come true! Actually, it wasn't, because back when I was playing basketball and football and running track, I couldn't even dream about something like that happening.

In high school, football wasn't even my favorite sport. My favorite sport was basketball and I thought I was going to play basketball at Northwest Missouri State University in Maryville. We were a small town, and I didn't think any big-time school or university knew anything about me. I know that no college coach ever scouted me or watched a King City game in person. My dad was the superintendent of schools in King City and he knew Sparky Stallcup, who was the athletic director at MU. I know he talked about me with Sparky a couple of times and shot him down some film, but I never thought anything about it. I was convinced I was going to Northwest. I was even thinking about running track, since I won the high and low hurdles and long jump at state my senior year.

Well, the next thing I know, a member of the MU football staff calls my coach at King City and they talk. Then my coach tells me that Missouri wants to offer me a scholarship.

Now, this is how different things were then, as compared to how recruiting goes today. I got a few form letters from Kansas State and Kansas – but they never came to see me play. Missouri never saw me play. This past year, as part of the Hall of Fame ceremony, we went to the Junior All-American Football Game in San Antonio, Texas. Now get this, it's just for high school juniors. Every great high school junior in the country is part of the game, and they treat them like kings. They go through all the testing the kids who have committed to the NFL draft go through and every big school in the nation is there – all of them. They time them in the 40, they do the vertical jump – everything. I couldn't believe it. And I got recruited over the phone, without ever being seen in person by any member of the coaching staff.

Looking back at my time at Missouri, it's pretty amazing how the dominoes began to fall. Missouri needed a defensive back, and that's the position I played. I fit in perfectly with Coach (Dan) Devine's defense and I was lucky enough to have a great career at MU with a great coach and teammates. People want to know how, if I was the team's shutdown corner, I could lead the Tigers with seven interceptions my senior year. I just tell them that offenses were different back when I played. Now, schools have the shot gun and the no huddle – back then, they just lined up and threw the ball to their best receiver. And I was usually covering that wide receiver. They say that a cornerback has to have a short memory, and I think that was one of my strengths. If I got beat, I just figured that I would be the receiver on the next play. I never let it play head games with me. I concentrated on the next play, and that was the only thing I concentrated on.

Going to MU was a real life-style change for a kid from a town of 1,003 people. I was Mr. Small Town, and now, I was on a campus with thousands of students and I was part of one of the best football teams in the country. I think the jump from King City to Columbia was a bigger jump than from the Tigers to the NFL's Cardinals. I was never away from home before I went to Columbia, and that was a big adjustment. But Coach Devine made every member of the team feel like he was a part of the football family. So I had my family in King City and my new family in Columbia, and that really helped. There were so many great memories that we would be here all day if I told you all of them. But I think going out my senior year with a win in the Gator Bowl over Alabama and Bear Bryant was about as special as it could get. We won the game, 35-10, but we just led about 10-7 at the half. I'd returned a punt for a touchdown right before the half, but it was called back because of a penalty, so it was still a very close game at halftime. I was thinking, "Gosh, we should be up by 20 points," and before long, we were. Our running back, Greg Cook, had a big second half and our defense just played great. Once you got to the fourth quarter, you would have never thought it was a close game – that's how dominating all phases of our game were in the second half.

What do they call duct tape in Manhattan?

Chrome.

My charmed life continued after college as I wound up being drafted by the St. Louis Cardinals. The Cardinals needed a defensive back and I was in St. Louis to get a college football award. I'd never been to St. Louis and the Cardinals coach, Charley Winner, came over to me and told me that the Cardinals might draft me. The draft was the next day and they drafted me. Like I said earlier, you know how different things are today. The NFL Draft is a big production on ESPN and back then, I got a call phone saying I had been drafted. I'd never been to St. Louis until the day before; now, I was going to call it my home. And I called it home for the next 14 years.

It was an honor to play for the Cardinals. I'm one of four Cardinals in the Pro Football Hall of Fame – along with Dan (Dierdorf), Jackie (Smith), and Larry (Wilson). I think that Roger Staubach's comment calling me the player most responsible for the term "shutdown corner" had a big impact on me making it into the Hall of Fame. A kid from King City is in the College Football Hall of Fame, the University of Missouri Hall of Fame, the Missouri (state) Hall of Fame, the Pro Football Hall of Fame, and St. Louis is working on a new Hall of Fame, and from what I understand, I'm going to be inducted into that, too. I could have never dreamed that big back when I was in King City. When I go back home, I see that sign that reads KING CITY, Population 1,003, and I just thank the good Lord that I came from a town like that and had great parents that taught me great values at a young age. I guess I couldn't have written a better script.

JOHN "NIPS" WEISENFELLS

University of Missouri linebacker, Class of 1970

Growing up in St. Louis in the 1960s, I watched Mizzou football and the exploits of Johnny Roland, Gus Otto, and Andy Russell. In those days, the high school football coaches in St. Louis all had ties to the Tigers. My coach was Ray Moss, who was the captain of the 1939 Mizzou team. So

> **If one of us was caught in town doing something we shouldn't be doing, the police didn't arrest us. Rather, they threatened to turn us over to Coach Devine. Most of us would have preferred the cops.**

when it came to a decision on what school I was going to attend, there wasn't much discussion.

Playing football at Mizzou was a great experience. My time there has impacted my life in so many ways since graduation. First of all, playing for Coach Dan Devine, you learned a lot about yourself. He believed his job was to set the bar of what was acceptable very high. He would push and push until you got it done. There were no excuses. It is funny how I look back to when I played and was kind of intimidated by him, but then after graduation you knew you could always count on him to help you out. In fact, it was because of his scholarship program for former players that I was able to afford to come back and get my law degree from Mizzou. I remember introducing him to my daughter and she asked me later why I said he was so tough. To her, he was the kindly grandpa type. He definitely wasn't that during a player's time at MU.

He was a great motivator and always knew what buttons to press to get us to play at a higher level. Many times he would come in at halftime and whip us into a frenzy, but not at the Gator Bowl in 1969. We had ended up there after a disappointing loss to Kansas. All the players voted to not even go to a bowl game, but he convinced us that the best thing was to go play in the Gator Bowl against Alabama. Well, all week leading up to the game all we heard from the media and fans was that we didn't stand a chance. They said we were nice boys, but this was Bear Bryant and Alabama. No one comes down south and beats the Bear.

After they returned an interception for a touchdown to start the game and then followed it up with a field goal, we thought maybe they were right. That is when the system of developing your seniors into leaders took hold. The seniors brought us together and we rallied for 14 straight points to lead at half. When Coach Devine walked in to address the team at halftime, he took one look around and saw how fired up we were and just walked out. We scored the first 21 points of the second half to put the game away.

He was such a strict disciplinarian that if one of us was caught in town doing something we shouldn't be doing the police didn't arrest us. Rather, they threatened to turn us over to Coach Devine. Most of us would have preferred the cops. However, he could be flexible. For example, when we played in the Gator Bowl, we practiced in Daytona Beach. The senior players went to him and negotiated that the players would be able to use some of the courtesy cars that the bowl committee provided to each team. It was a great time, practicing in the sun and then hanging out on the beach at night. In the end, we all were at our best mentally and physically come game time.

Mizzou fans know about the half of a piece sign that Kansas Coach Pepper Rogers said Devine gave him, but there was another story that took place during that game. KU running back John Riggins was a force during his college career. On that day he was outmanned and he knew it. Late in the fourth quarter with the game pretty much decided, he continued to run the ball. And we continued to pound him with gang tackles. After one such play you could hear Riggins at the bottom of the pile. As the players were lying on top of him, Riggins told us that he was having a party at his house after the game and we were all invited. Laughing as we got up, I wondered if Devine would let me go home with friends. Riggins was a true competitor, but on this day he was trying to make peace. As far as Devine letting me go home with friends, I knew that wasn't going to happen. I appreciated the offer and hit him again on the next play.

Years later I relived another football memory courtesy of a Michigan fan. My daughter was a student at the University of Michigan. (I would pay for my kids to go to any college except Kansas. I thought that was fair.) One Saturday we went to a game in the Big House and I sat next to a long-time season ticket holder. Upon learning that I played at Mizzou, he proceeded to give me a play-by-play breakdown of the game I had played in at the Big House back in 1969. Since we won that game, I didn't mind hearing about it again.

My love for Mizzou remains strong as I have had season tickets since the 1970s and my brother and sister followed me there.

JON SUNDVOLD

MU was 100-28 during Sundvold's four years at the university and he was all-conference, all-district, and all-Big 8 twice and an All-America in 1983.

When I think back to my playing days at Missouri, the first things I think about are Coach (Norm) Stewart and all my great teammates. Then I think about how we won the four conference championships in a row. Every team was so different, and so special. And the older I get, the more special each team becomes. When I went to Missouri, we didn't just talk about winning a championship each year, we really thought we could do it. And that confidence came from Coach Stewart, who really believed in each one of us.

The first Big 8 championship was fun. It was exciting. I was a kid from Blue Springs, Missouri, playing for Missouri, and I was having the time of my life. When we won the Big 8 championship I thought how great it would be to do something like that every year. Little did I know . . .

The second championship was a bit of a surprise. We weren't supposed to win it. But no one told Coach Stewart or the team that we weren't supposed to win. We were very good my junior year and everyone picked us to win for a third year in a row – and we did. Then, my senior year, OU was the team everyone was talking about. We had the two All-America candidates in me and Stipo (Steve Stipanovich, who shared each Big 8 championship with Sundvold) but Oklahoma had Wayman Tisdale and all anyone was talking or writing about was OU. Billy Tubbs made a few comments that helped our cause, as if we needed any additional motivation. We were in a tournament in Hawaii and we beat North Carolina. OU was also in the tournament and we watched some of their practice. We watched them run sprints, and let's just say, they didn't exactly run sprints the way Coach Stewart had us run sprints. We just thought, "There's no way we're going to let those guys beat us." We played a slow-down game. Coach Stewart had a great game plan and we beat them at our place and at their place. Coach told us they were a running team, but that "they didn't run back on defense." I don't think anyone thought we were going to win that fourth championship except our fans and the guys in the locker room. It might have been the most special of the four.

When I think of MU basketball, I immediately think of Coach Stewart. The man never took a day off from coaching, and he didn't expect his players to take a day off, either. Whether you were a walk-on or an All-America, you didn't take a day off. I understood how badly he wanted to win, because I wanted to win that badly, too. Some kids who played for Coach had to battle their egos. Some thought they could beat anyone, but when they played for Coach, they found out that they had better become team players. Coach loved to recruit players from Missouri. He once said, "I don't coach McDonald's All-Americas. My kids just eat at McDonald's." He didn't get the big-name All-Americas, but he got hard-working kids and made them into All-America candidates. And unless you were a part of the team, you never knew how hard he worked or how much he cared for his team. There were times I disagreed with Coach. But in the end, his way was the best way to get things done. And doing it his way usually resulted in an MU victory.

I think one reason Coach was always taking on the media or fans from other teams is because he wanted the attention to be focused on him, rather than on a bunch of 18-, 19- or 20-year-olds. He loved the attention, anyway. He was always the target of the opposing fans; it was never us, it was Coach. He was smart that way. We'd walk out to the court before a game in Nebraska and the first thing you'd hear was the student section yelling, "Sit down, Norm!" He just smiled.

At Iowa State, Stipo does a ball fake – he did it all the time – but he accidentally hit Iowa State's Lefty Moore in the forehead. (Iowa State coach) Johnny Orr had that high-pitched voice, and he starts screaming at our team and at Coach Stewart. He wants a technical foul. He's just screaming and screaming at the officials. It got pretty loud in Hilton Coliseum and during a time out, Coach takes us off the bench and out on the court. Some guy comes running down the aisle behind our bench and starts cussing at Stipo. I mean, he's yelling and screaming and cussing and Coach just looks right through us and starts cussing right back. Coach cusses him up one side and down the other and uses cuss words in combinations that I had never heard and probably will never hear again. Coach was defending his player and his team. It was Coach against that one crazy fan and 15,000 other Iowa State fans – and he won. While all this was going on, I looked behind our bench and there were my parents and grandparents. They heard it all. Coach asked my brother, Bob, an assistant coach on the team, who was sitting behind our bench and he said, "My parents and grandparents." Coach wrote them a note, apologizing for his language and thanking them for their support. My parents and grandparents thought the world of Coach and they knew what he was doing that afternoon. He was taking the pressure away from his team and protecting his players. Even though he did it in a colorful fashion that none of us really expected.

Coach took a bunch of kids who were mainly from Missouri and went out and beat the North Carolinas and the

> Did you hear about the fire in the K-State football dorm? It destroyed dozens of books.
>
> The real tragedy is that about 10 of them hadn't been colored in yet.

North Carolina States. We played Georgetown and any big-time program Coach could get on the schedule. I think playing competition like that helped both me and Stipo get drafted in the NBA. We were tough mentally and physically and we were used to playing the best college teams and players and that prepared us to take our game to the next level. As a kid, I dreamed of playing in the NBA. That was crazy. Kids from Blue Springs don't play in the NBA. My brothers worked as hard as I did and they played juco ball. When there was talk that I was going to be drafted, Coach just told me, "You are good enough to play at the next level. Just do what you do well and play as hard for them as you have for me and you'll be fine." He taught me a lot about basketball, but he also taught me life lessons that were even more important.

I also have to say how special it was to play at Hearnes and play before our fans. We didn't lose a lot of games at home and our fans had a lot to do with that. The Antlers were crazy. They would taunt an opposing player or taunt the entire team and Coach loved that. I questioned some of their tactics, but they were great for the team. They made it tough for our opponents, and that's what Coach loved about them. From the moment Coach walked out onto the floor, which was right before the game when we started our shoot-around, he owned the place. The fans loved Coach and he loved them right back.

DERRICK CHIEVOUS

Missouri's all-time leading scorer

When I came to Mizzou, I was only 17 years old and it was a long way from New York City. Talk about culture shock! I had actually visited Kansas first, but didn't like it in Lawrence. So when Coach (Rich) Daly came to see me and had me visit, I was sold on the University and Columbia. I had found a new home.

Playing for Coach (Norm) Stewart, we soon found out that you went into every game knowing you were prepared and that nobody was going to play harder than the Tigers. One thing that I am very proud of is that we only lost two games at home in my four years playing in the Hearnes Center.

I can remember Oklahoma coming to Columbia my freshman year. Billy Tubbs was their coach and their star was Wayman Tisdale. The place was electric and when I got the chance to dunk on Tisdale the place exploded. Here I was, a 17-year-old freshman and he was the star of the Big 8. We sent a message that day.

I loved the fans in Columbia, but my favorites were the Antlers. That crazy group was the best at getting under the opponent's skin. And what most people don't know is that they rehearsed and practiced just like they were preparing for a performance. The best show they put on was when they made fun of Billy Tubbs when he got hit by a car while jogging. They had a guy driving a little plastic car and another one playing the part of Tubbs. It was like a "Saturday Night Live" skit – only better. I always appreciated their support for us.

COLIN BROWN

University of Missouri offensive lineman and a fifth-round draft pick of the Kansas City Chiefs

Growing up, I always followed Mizzou football, but my last two years of high school I kind of lost track of how they were doing. During that time, I was busy focusing on basketball and football and hoping that I would ultimately be able to get a scholarship to play basketball somewhere. Other than Brad Smith, Coach (Gary) Pinkel, and a couple of other players, I really didn't know very much about Tiger football when I showed up to campus in 2004.

Game day is kind of a hard topic for me to talk about, because I don't remember much about it. It took me three seasons to get the chance to play a meaningful snap, so the last thing I wanted to do was screw it up. My entire focus was on making sure that I never let my guy touch Chase (Daniel) and that I opened holes for the running game. I still remember almost every time that I gave up a hit on the quarterback, and there were times I wouldn't sleep much for a day or two if I let Chase get touched. Tiger Walk, while most players really enjoyed it, was one of my least favorite parts of game day. I didn't want to see or talk to anybody before the game, so on that walk I would keep my head down until I got to the area where my parents were waiting for me.

What do you call a good-looking girl on the KU campus?

A visitor.

I would give them a hug and then try and get to the locker room as soon as I could. Once I got to the locker room, I always felt a lot better because I knew the distractions were over, and from there I had a set routine that I followed every week. I would listen to the same songs on my iPod every week, read the program, and then get dressed. I got my thumbs taped and drank a glass of pickle juice right before warmups – and then it was on.

Draft day was a very nervous time. Since I was little, I had always dreamed of playing in the NFL. There were some anxious moments in the weeks leading up to the draft. I had been told by my agent that there was about a 50-50 chance that I would get drafted in the fifth round or later, but we really didn't have any clear idea what teams were interested. As draft day got closer, the more nervous I got that I wasn't going to be picked and that my NFL dreams might be over before they started. I stayed in Columbia the day and night of the first and second rounds because I didn't want to have to go home and think about it or answer questions from people that I hadn't seen in a while. I remember waking up early on Sunday of the second day of the draft, wondering what was going to happen. My dad had been charting where all of the offensive lineman had gone. That way, if I didn't get drafted, we would know which situations looked better based off what each team had drafted. As it turned out, it didn't really matter. I remember (Kansas City Chiefs) Coach Maurice Carthon called me from a blocked number and asked me how I was doing, made sure I was still healthy and had not gotten into any trouble lately, and based off of the questions, I just thought he was a scout checking in to tell me they were interested and might draft me later on. I remember he made the statement that I didn't sound very excited, even though I assured him I was. I just didn't realize what was happening. Then when he said he was going to let me talk to Coach (Todd) Haley, I knew my dreams were about to come true. Coach Haley told me that they were going to turn in the card and in about 10 seconds I would be a Kansas City Chief, and I swear that was the longest period of time as I waited to watch it show up on the screen to know it was for sure. After that, I know I talked to Scott Pioli and Clark Hunt and the media, but I have no idea what was said. I was so stunned and had so many emotions running through my mind and my phone was going crazy from all of the text and phone calls I was receiving that it seemed like time was in slow motion.

The Chiefs have always been my favorite team growing up, and to get a chance to actually play for them was a dream come true.

ROGER PHILLIPS

University of Missouri guard and linebacker, Class of 1962

I came to Mizzou at the beginning of our best decade of football. Playing for Coach (Dan) Devine was an experience I won't forget. He was a master motivator who drove all of us to be the best. However, if it wasn't for a couple of close friends and a summer workout, I may have missed it all.

While playing football at Southeast High School in Kansas City, I was recruited by both Kansas State and Missouri. Back in those days, you had different levels of scholarships. There were full scholarships and half scholarships. When push came to shove, I committed to Kansas State because they offered me a full scholarship. Missouri had only offered to pay my tuition and books. My parents didn't have a lot of money, so I thought it best to commit to Kansas State.

During the summer prior to my enrollment, I worked out with three friends that were also football players. Bud Abel, Conrad Hitchler, and Bo Newman were all going to Mizzou. By the second week of workouts, I started thinking that I really didn't want to go to K-State and play against these guys. So one day I called the freshmen coach, Harry Smith, and asked if the scholarship offer at Mizzou was still available. When he told me it was, I told him that I wanted to be a Tiger.

> **"We will go down as one of the few undefeated teams in college football to not earn a National Championship."**

That led me to Columbia and some of the best times of my life. I also became lifelong friends with Bud Abel and many of my teammates. While there, I played both ways. Believe it or not, I was an offensive guard and a linebacker. We ran a lot of power sweeps so Devine liked his guards to be able to run. I wasn't the biggest guy out there, but I could run. Of course, it was easy to gain yards when you had backs like Mel West, Norris Stephenson, and, later, Johnny Roland.

During my sophomore year, we upset Oklahoma and were ranked No. 1 in the country. It was a fun time to be a Tiger, albeit short-lived. I remember coming back from the game and the airport was packed with fans cheering us on. We had great fans in those days – more students than adults during that time. Unfortunately, the following week was Thanksgiving week, and we were left all alone on campus to prepare for our final game with Kansas.

Talk about going from the ultimate high to a big let-down! We lost to a very good Kansas team, but then went on to beat

Navy in the Orange Bowl. Only after the game did we find out that Kansas used an illegal player. The game was ruled a forfeit and we were awarded the win. So after we held the great Joe Bellino from Navy to negative yardage in the Orange Bowl, we were undefeated. However, back in those days, it was a vote for the National Championship. We will go down as one of the few undefeated teams in college football to not earn a National Championship.

JARON BASTON

University of Missouri, senior defensive captain

Game day at Faurot Field: Is there anything better? In high school, I loved Friday nights under the lights. I didn't think there was anything better – until I got to Missouri. Now, nothing tops Saturday afternoon at Faurot Field. It's electric. You can feel the electricity cracking and popping. It all starts building on Friday night, when we stay in a local hotel. That gets us thinking about one thing, and only one thing – football. The next day we get on the bus, drive to campus, get ready for the game, and begin the Tiger Walk. I love it when the fans pound on my shoulder pads or call out my name. When we had Pig Brown, the fans would bring all sorts of pig mascots. With Ziggy Hood, they'd bring the Ziggy characters. I think I'm kind of known as the team's high energy guy and the walk gets me fired up.

When we get in the stadium and the fans start cheering and screaming, you can't even hear the person standing next to you. I remember my first game and I wasn't even playing. I was a freshman and I was thinking how incredible it would be, to be a part of a big-time Division I game. Now, I know what that's like. I can remember back when Nebraska or OU would come to town and there would be so many Nebraska or OU fans in the stands you wondered where our fans were. Well, that doesn't happen any more. You don't see any of that red and white stuff. You see the black and gold – a whole lot of black and gold. And we notice that. We hear you screaming and cheering, we see the school colors, and that just makes us want to play that much harder.

When you watch me playing, when you watch me yelling and screaming, even though I'm tired, that's what being a Tiger means to me. This is my fifth year, my last year. I want to go out and do a lot of things during the season and after this season.

Me and Spoon (teammate Sean Weatherspoon) talked about this year after that bowl game (Alamo Bowl). We knew it was going to be our senior year and our time, and we were probably most likely going to be the leaders on the defense. We wanted to put our personalities in the defense, and that's more of a loud, have fun, be loose, but still be focused at the same time. I think the younger guys and some of the role-playing guys are starting to pick that up.

My mindset now is to believe in myself and I want the other guys on the team, especially the younger guys, to believe in themselves. It used to be, "What if this happened? What if that happened?" It's more relaxed, a "just enjoy the moment" type of feel now. Listen to some music; just get ready to go, man.

And after the game, nothing is better than going into downtown Columbia and sharing the victory with the fans – especially the student body. You get to let them reap the benefits of a hard week of practice and share the moment with you and your teammates. Some guys like to just be by themselves after a game, but I'm the type of guy who wants to share the big-game atmosphere with everyone on campus. I love it here, I feel blessed, and I want everyone to experience that feeling.

JEFF HANDY

Before Brad Smith and Chase Daniel, Handy was the most decorated quarterback in the history of Missouri. When he graduated in 1995, he held 25 Mizzou passing records.

It's funny looking back on my high school career. I was recruited by a lot of schools. At the peak of the recruiting period, I probably got 10 letters a day from schools all over the country. Some were personal, hand-written letters from coaches, and others were the form letters that they sent so you would know they were still thinking about you. It was pretty amazing for a kid from Blue Springs, Missouri, to get that much attention. I read every letter and talked to a lot of coaches, but deep down inside I knew I was going to Missouri. I thought a little bit about going to Illinois because they were really interested in me. But my dad was a big Mizzou fan and when they asked me to become a Tiger, I couldn't say no. I liked Coach (Bob) Stull and he had a great young staff. I like to think that back when I played, we laid the foundation for the great teams to come with guys like Brad Smith and Chase Daniel.

It's hard for people to believe now, but we couldn't get 50,000 fans to come watch us play. They would fill the stadium for teams like Nebraska and Oklahoma, but that's because it was the Nebraska and Oklahoma fans coming to Columbia. All their home games would sell out, so they had to go on the road to see their team. But all I cared about was having my mom and dad in the stands – and they were always there to support me.

Looking back at my time at Mizzou, there are so many memories, but there are a few games that just stick out in my mind. The first one, I didn't even play in. I was a freshman and was standing on the sidelines of the fifth-down game against Colorado. I still don't know how all the officials missed the fifth down because everyone on our sidelines knew what was happening. Our defensive coordinator was screaming out, "That's fifth down." We tried to count the plays in our heads and we all counted five – and then they give Colorado the touchdown and he never made it into the end zone. We're standing there in disbelief. What just happened? Can we appeal? We're in the locker room and no one is throwing chairs or doing anything crazy, but all the coaches are talking, like, "What just happened and what can be done?" Well, nothing was done and it was just as crazy a scene as I've ever seen on a football field.

Another special moment came my senior year, but it didn't happen on the football field. I went with other representatives of the school to the Big 8 Media Day. We went to Kansas City and St. Louis and all the big-time coaches were there. Dan Devine was with our group and the whole time we were on the trip he carried a sack with a football inside. At first, I thought it was a Nerf football, something he was going to toss to a fan. He has that sack the entire time. When we get back to Columbia, Coach Devine comes over to me and says, "Jeff, I have something for you."

And he hands me the sack. I open it up and it's a special Notre Dame football signed by Ara Parseghian. To this day, I don't know why he gave it to me. But when he handed me the ball, he said, "Jeff, I wish I could have coached you while I was at Missouri." That was one of the best compliments I ever received. I still have that football in a trophy case in my home.

ANTHONY PEELER

University of Missouri and NBA great

Coming out of high school, I had my pick of just about any college in the country. My five visits included Kansas, Maryland, Oklahoma, Syracuse, and Missouri. It was a tough choice until Coach (Norm) Stewart broke it down for me. Having played in Kansas City and established my name in the area over the four years I was in high school, he said that by coming to Missouri, I could build on that name recognition. He was right and I signed with the Tigers.

There were some great times during my career at Mizzou, but there were also some scary times. I remember winning at Kansas my freshman year and everyone jumping around like we had won a National Championship. It was at that point I really understood the rivalry.

There was another Kansas game that I remember just as well. We were flying to Lawrence my senior year and I was told on the airplane that Byron Houston from Oklahoma State was going to be named the (Big 8) Player of the Year. Hearing this, it gave me additional motivation for my final game against the Jayhawks. Beating Kansas and showing the rest of the Big 8 that I was the best player in the league would be the best way to go out. That day we came up short in Lawrence, but I did score 43 points and proved my ability to anyone who doubted me. Of course, I would have loved to get the win, as well.

The scary part was flying to the game at Oklahoma. Coach Stewart was on the plane, but he wasn't his normal self. He usually played cards on the flights to games, but this time he just sat there. Suddenly, he fell ill on the plane and the pilot had to make an emergency landing in Stillwater. We left Coach Stewart at the hospital and proceeded to the game. It was a match up of No. 1 vs. No. 2 with Coach (Rich) Daly serving as the head coach in his first game. Most of us were recruited by him so we all wanted to do our best for him. However, it was difficult to concentrate knowing that Coach Stewart was back in the hospital. It was later that we were told that Coach Stewart had cancer. This affected the whole team. Coach was a player's coach and he really was like a father figure. He treated you with respect and helped you grow as a man. Thank goodness he came through it.

Another aspect of playing at Mizzou was what the Antlers did to opponents. I didn't know the full extent of their assistance until I started playing in the NBA and talked with some of the guys whose teams played us. Todd Day from Arkansas told me how he would get mail the week before the game with Missouri. Thinking it was fan mail, he would open it. It turned out to be letters from the Antlers telling him what was in store for him and his team once they got to Columbia. To this day I always wondered how they got opposing players' addresses. Then again, to be a part of the Antlers you had to have at least a 3.6 GPA, so they definitely were smart enough to figure out a way to get to our opponents. And once the opposing team arrived in Columbia, they went to work calling their hotel rooms and having pizza delivered to them at all hours of the night.

My time at Mizzou was a great experience because of my teammates, the coaches, and fans.

CHASE DANIEL

University of Missouri quarterback, who was a two-time Heisman Trophy candidate, is Missouri's all-time total yardage leader (13,256)

I loved playing football at Missouri. I loved everything about it, from opening the season against Illinois – which was like a bowl game, complete with fireworks – to playing miniature golf with my buddies down the road from Faurot Field.

When we won 12 games my junior year, the campus went crazy. We won like six or seven in a row, and then beat Kansas, and the place exploded – I mean, with the band, cheerleaders, Golden Girls, the drum corps, our crazy fans – it was unbelievable. It would be great if everyone, at one time in their life, could experience something like the members of the football team experienced that year. And we enjoyed sharing it with the fans. I had a lot going on that year, balancing school, and football, and all the other stuff that went with the type of year the team had. It was difficult at times, but I knew it was one of those once-in-a-lifetime experiences and I made sure that I enjoyed every minute of it. Really, I mean this, it was the best time of my life.

People ask me about the 12-win season, how we did it, what it was like to be in the hunt for the Heisman (Trophy), and I tell them we just took each game one at a time. We took each practice one at a time. We took each play – in practice and in games – one play at a time. I know that's a vanilla answer, and it's not the answer most people expect to hear, but it's the truth. We had so many great players, so many great teammates, it was just an amazing experience for the team and the university and the city of Columbia.

People also want to know how I got out of Texas, since I'm from Southlake, and Texas is such a football-crazy state. I made an unofficial visit to Missouri before my senior year, and once I got here, I knew this was the place for me. I made other visits, to Stanford and Oklahoma State, but once I stepped foot on this campus and met the coaches and the guys on the team, I knew Missouri was where I was going to go to college and play football. Columbia reminded me of my hometown and Missouri was the first school to make an offer. When things got crazy, and offers were coming in from everywhere, I wanted to reward Missouri for always being there for me, so I made the commitment to come to Missouri, and it was one of the best decisions of my life.

WINSTON WRIGHT

Former standout running back from Blue Springs South High School, who is now a freshman in the University of Missouri secondary

I am humbled and honored and blessed to be a part of the Missouri football team. I can say my dreams have come true.

And I don't know of too many people who can make that statement.

Winston Wright

Photo courtesy of Jim Dalton

I had a lot of offers for full rides from some smaller schools, but there is where I wanted to play. I imagined playing in front of a packed house against a big rival like Kansas or Texas or Oklahoma. I would close my eyes and I could see the crowd and feel the excitement. When I walked on, I wanted to make an immediate impact. I knew the coaches had high expectations for all the players, but they couldn't have had any higher expectations than I had for myself.

I was a running back in high school, but I made this team as a member of the defensive secondary. I played some cornerback in high school, and I feel like I always played offense with a defensive mind set – I wanted to hit those guys as hard as they were hitting me. As the practice sessions went on, I did everything I could to make an impact, to get noticed by the coaches. Finally, one day my position coach came up to me and said, "Welcome to the team." What a feeling. I can't even describe how I felt. I just thanked God and called my family to tell them.

I'm not going to let anything disturb this dream, because every day that I come to practice I feel like all my dreams have come true.

BILL McCARTNEY

University of Missouri Class of 1962, coached Colorado to a National Championship in 1990, and founded the Christian men's group Promise Keepers

As I reflect on my playing days at Mizzou, I'm reminded of the rivalry with the Jayhawks. My freshman year (at that time, freshmen could not compete on the varsity level), our frosh team was instructed to defend the goal posts if we lost the game. Well, we lost! And the KU football team charged the end zones, overpowered us, and took the posts down. From that time on, I understood the importance and significance of the game. Today, at the age of 69, I want every Missouri Tiger to defend the goal posts by winning the games at home. I'm still waiting for us to take their posts down in Lawrence.

GARY BARNETT

University of Missouri Class of 1968, who went on to coach at Northwestern and Colorado

Growing up in Mexico, Missouri, and then in St. Louis, football was life in Missouri. When I came to play football at Mizzou, it was a tremendous opportunity. I played for Coach Dan Devine and made lifelong relationships with many of the coaches and built tight bonds with my teammates.

The one thing that sticks out in my mind is the great respect that everyone had for all those who were associated with the football program. It was not only for the players, but the cheerleaders and the band members, as well. On Saturdays in the fall, it was the thing to do. Everyone would

> **"One practice I will never forget is the day the wife of one of our seniors baked a huge chocolate cake filled with ex-lax and delivered it to the coaches' office. They went after that cake like they hadn't eaten in a week."**

get dressed up and go to the games. Back then, guys would wear a coat and tie to a game. It was just a different type of atmosphere in Columbia.

One practice I will never forget is the day the wife of one of our seniors, Donnie Nelson, baked a huge chocolate cake filled with ex-lax and delivered it to the coaches' office. They went after that cake like they hadn't eaten in a week.

Midway through practice, the assistant coaches started excusing themselves and heading for the locker room. It got to the point where there were not enough coaches left on the field so Coach Devine cut practice short.

As the coach at Colorado, I brought my teams (to Columbia) 15 times and won all but two. Those were great wins for us, but it was always tough to beat your alma mater. Once a Tiger, always a Tiger.

BILL WHITAKER

University of Missouri Class of 1980

I went to Mizzou games to watch my brother play when I was a youngster. He was 14 years older than me, but his playing there made a lasting impression on me. However, when it came time for my senior year in high school, I had to choose between Notre Dame and Missouri. This created a very unusual situation.

By that time my brother's coach at Mizzou, Dan Devine, had moved on to Notre Dame. Coach Devine pulled out all the stops by having my brother there in South Bend when I made my visit to Notre Dame. In the end, though, I really liked the idea of playing at Mizzou.

However, I just couldn't get away from Coach Devine. The opening game my sophomore year (my first year playing full-time on the varsity) was at Notre Dame. They were coming into the game as the defending National Champion. Prior to the game, Coach Devine came over to me and said, "It's too bad you didn't come to Notre Dame. You would have had a championship ring." Well, we played a great game that day and ended up winning, 3-0. After the game, I almost ran over to Devine to talk some trash, but out of respect to him, and to my brother, I resisted.

That was the beginning of an unbelievable year. During the course of the year, we would play Illinois and Alabama outside of the conference, in addition to Notre Dame. Our last game was at Nebraska. They were ranked No. 1 in the country and we were a 28-point underdog. We pulled off the upset and put bookend wins on the board that I don't think any other team has matched. We beat the No.1 team in the country in the opener and did it again in the last game. Then just for good measure, we went down to Memphis and beat LSU in the Liberty Bowl. It was the first of three straight bowls that I would be fortunate enough to go to as a player at Mizzou.

CHAPTER 3

We Love the Game

From the man who has the scoreboard from the old
stadium in his basement to the fan who buried his father
in his MU gear, this chapter is about the fanatics who
bleed black and gold.

CONGRESSMAN SAM GRAVES

University of Missouri class of 1986

Congressman Sam Graves
Photo courtesy of Congressman
Sam Graves

My blood lines to Missouri go back to my great grandfather. We are Mizzou people through and through. My father, both brothers, sister, and their spouses all went to Missouri. Now my daughter goes there and my other two kids will go there, as well.

When I was in school, I belonged to the Alpha Gamma Sigma fraternity. We had a tradition (and still do today) that each weekend there was a home football game, we would host the alumni from the fraternity. That meant on Friday you had clean-up duty of the house and the yard. Then everyone who lived in the house moved their cars to another parking lot so that the alumni had a place to park. At the time I was not thrilled with this, but now that I go back as an alum I enjoy having a close parking place.

The alumni would start pulling in on Saturday morning and the tailgating would begin shortly thereafter. There was a tremendous sense of camaraderie amongst the current members and the alumni. This fellowship permeated the group throughout the games, win or lose. Then after the game we would head down to a place that became known as the "Party Barn."

Our fraternity was also front-and-center at the basketball games. Thanks to one of our members, Steve Knorr, who was on the student board, we were always able to get great seats.

I have been going to Mizzou football and basketball games for as long as I can remember. Our family has many cherished memories and mementos of the Tigers. My father even has a piece of the goal post from the 1956 win over Kansas. I am not sure what side of the goal post he was on when it came down in celebration of the win that day.

GEOFF HILL

University of Missouri Class of 1992, former Sports Information Director at the University of Missouri-Kansas City.

My four years at Missouri as a student, 1988-92, may have been one of the most unique and memorable four-year stretches that any student has ever witnessed at the university.

During that era, I had the privilege of serving as a student assistant in the sports information department under the direction of Sports Information Director Bob Brendel and his assistant, Jack Watkins. They taught me so much about the business of intercollegiate athletics and were fun to be around on a personal level.

I'll never forget walking into the sports information office on my first day as a freshman. A nervous teenager, I introduced myself to the staff and noticed a photo of the Antlers hanging on the wall in Brendel's office. It was a classic shot of the Antlers holding up three signs: the one on the left was a drawing of Kansas coach Larry Brown; the one on the right was a drawing of Libyan dictator Moammar Khadafy; and the sign in the middle simply asked, "Which one is Khadafy?" Welcome to Mizzou.

During my four years, a lot of unusual things happened. There was the fifth down game. A football coach was fired (Woody Widenhofer) and hired (Bob Stull). A Big 8 basketball championship was celebrated in 1990, and two Big 8 Tournament titles were won in Kansas City in 1989 and 1991. And don't forget about a No. 1 basketball ranking in the major polls for several weeks during the winter of 1990. But there was also the NCAA investigation into the basketball program that turned up major infractions, resulting in the loss of assistant coaches, a postseason tournament ban, and the reduction of scholarships. It was a wild ride and a tremendous personal experience for me, despite the lows.

Five downs?

How in the world can you win or lose a game with five downs? It could only happen to Missouri. In 1990, the Tigers had Colorado, a national champion contender, on the ropes and scrambling to save its title hopes on a sunny afternoon in Columbia. The Buffaloes were in their hurry-up offense in the final seconds of the fourth quarter under the direction of Charles Johnson at quarterback. They desperately needed a touchdown to avoid a loss to the Tigers.

Look at the facts.

1st down and Goal—the ball was spiked by quarterback Charles Johnson to stop the clock.

2nd down and Goal—Eric Bienemy's rush was stopped short of the goal line and Colorado was forced to call a timeout to stop the clock.

3rd down and Goal—Bienemy rushed the ball and again fell short of the end zone.

4th down and Goal—Johnson spiked the ball with two seconds remaining on the clock. But for some reason, the whole world lost track of the downs on this series and thought this play had been third down. It really was fourth down and Colorado had just turned the ball over to Missouri. Right? Wrong!

Fifth down and Goal – Johnson reaches across the goal line as time expires to take a two-point lead. The play should never have happened. But the ironic thing is that the play would have likely been reviewed in today's world of instant replay to determine if he really made it into the end zone. I'm not entirely sure he actually scored on the play, but the officials were very gracious and signaled a touchdown.

Despite the slow touchdown call by the officials, the Missouri fans in the student section began to rush the field to celebrate. The goal posts were beginning to come down.

And then there was mass confusion at Faurot Field. The Buffaloes were told by their coaches to head to the locker room. The game officials huddled. A simple mistake, most likely an innocent mistake made by the person operating the down marker on the field, became much more compounded at this point.

What happened?

The thing that I remember most from the chaos as I was sitting in the press box keeping statistics is that nobody knew it was actually five downs. Nobody. Not the coaches from either team, not the referees on the field, not the fans in the stadium, not the members of the media covering the game in the press box, and not the television announcers. And anybody that claims to know the downs were incorrect after the fact should be questioned as to why they remained silent throughout the series of plays. Oh sure, you'll find somebody to claim they were in attendance and spout off that they really "knew" it was five downs. Don't believe them.

The one thing, yes a thing and not a person, that "knew" it was five downs was the in-game computerized statistics program. This was the beginning age of in-game computerized statistics. For years dating back to the game's invention, statistics were recorded manually by pencil and paper, but the computer age was upon

❝There was a classic shot of the Antlers holding up three signs: the one on the left was a drawing of Kansas coach Larry Brown; the one on the right was a drawing of Libyan dictator Moammar Khadafy; and the sign in the middle simply asked, "Which one is Khadafy?❞

us. I was two seats to the right of the stat monitor that "knew" about the five downs.

The last series of plays went by fast, so fast that the person responsible for entering the statistical codes on the keyboard did not actually look at the computer screen, as all eyes were glued to the action on the field. Why wasn't the computer allowing the stat crew to enter the touchdown scoring play? The screen simply read "Missouri ball, first down, on the one-yard line." What? How did that happen?

Our first reaction on the stat crew was to question ourselves. Did we do something wrong? Did we make a mistake entering the play? And then after what seemed to be at least 10 minutes, but probably was only about 60 seconds, one of the members of the stat crew loudly yelled "That was five downs!"

And then everybody in the area literally wanted to scream, "Oh _____ (insert your favorite word of profanity here)!"

I remember the game officials calling upstairs to the press box trying to reach the stand-by official for direction, which so very rarely occurred during this era of college football. But the official had vacated the press box to head down to the field with Big 8 Commissioner Carl James. It was very common for school and conference administrators, along with the media, to clear the press box with about five minutes remaining in the fourth quarter. It was necessary if you wanted to be a part of the post-game interview process for coaches and student-athletes. Seems crazy, but Faurot Field has the slowest elevator on the planet.

Those of us on the stat crew, and about half of the reporters, remained in the press box to watch the conclusion of the game. Because the game officials could not communicate with anybody upstairs, they had no choice but to let the touchdown stand.

The awkwardness continued. Since the game score was only a two-point differential, the players from both teams were ordered back onto the field to try the extra point with no time left on the game clock. Crazy? Theoretically, Missouri could have blocked an extra point try and run the ball back for a two-point conversion that would have tied the game. But Colorado was too smart for this and simply took a knee to escape with a two-point 33-31 victory.

The other memory that stands out from the fifth down game was that the Big 8 commissioner could not be found following the aftermath. Naturally, the press wanted to speak with Carl James for his reaction, but he decided it was better to get on the road for the short drive to Kansas City. The game officials were later suspended, but the result stood. Colorado wins, Missouri loses.

Unfortunately, that was the most excitement we had in football, but the heat really turned up during basketball season.

> **"One of the members of the stat crew loudly yelled "That was five downs!" And then everybody in the area literally wanted to scream, "Oh _____ (insert your favorite word of profanity here)!""**

I'll always remember the great basketball games with Illinois in St. Louis. The Arena was such a great venue for this event, and I don't think the game has quite been the same since it moved to the new facility.

As exciting and competitive as the games were, for some reason Illinois seemed to beat us a lot. Try December 19, 1988, as fifth-ranked Illinois knocked off 10th-ranked Missouri, 87-84. It was the sixth straight loss to the Illini in the series. We went on to make the Sweet 16 while Illinois advanced to the Final Four. On that December night, the floor was loaded with future NBA talent. For Mizzou, we had Byron Irvin, Gary Leonard, Doug Smith, and Anthony Peeler. We were good, but they were better.

"Don't worry, fellas, the altitude only affects you outdoors and our game is indoors."

My freshman year was made for Hollywood. Following the close encounter with Illinois, we jumped off to a great start and stood in first place in the Big 8 halfway through the season. But then, Norm Stewart got sick on the plane ride to Norman, Oklahoma, for a game on ESPN against the Sooners. Earlier on that same day, assistant coach Bob Sundvold was suspended for violating NCAA rules. Rich Daly coached the team that night as the national television audience got to see OU coach Billy Tubbs take the public address announcer's microphone. He pleaded with the Sooner fans, calmly stating, "Regardless of how terrible the officiating is, do not throw stuff on the court"! Tubbs got a technical, but it was hilarious, and Oklahoma went on to win the game.

Norm Stewart was diagnosed with colon cancer later that week and did not coach the rest of the 1989 season. I do remember that he called press row from the hospital at halftime during a home game later in the season, asking to speak with the graduate assistant on the basketball staff to pass along advice to Coach Daly in the locker room. Fighting for his life against cancer, he could still help coach the Tigers from his hospital bed and a television set. He is one of the toughest individuals I've ever had the privilege to meet, and his teams resembled that grit and determination on and off the court.

I remember Coach Daly at his best. One time before a practice, he noticed the players were doing routine stretching exercises, but a few of them seemed concerned about something. He walked over and asked Lee Coward what they were pondering. Coward looked up at Coach Daly and informed him that he was not looking forward to playing in the high altitude at Colorado. Coach Daly responded with wisdom and said, "Don't worry, fellas, the altitude only affects you outdoors and our game is indoors." Problem solved.

We went on to finish a close second in the Big 8 during the 1989 regular season to Oklahoma. But we easily handled the Sooners in the championship game of the Big 8 Tournament at Kansas City's Kemper Arena, dominating them in front of a very pro- Missouri crowd. I'm convinced that this team was the best that Missouri has ever put on the basketball floor. If only Coach Stewart had not gotten sick, we just might have had our first Final Four.

As a sophomore, another personal memory came against Illinois in St. Louis. This time, fifth-ranked Illinois edged fourth-ranked Mizzou, 101-93, in a hard-fought battle on December 20, 1989, our seventh straight loss to the Illini. As I proceeded to walk with Coach Stewart to the media room, I'll never forget what happened next. Coach Stewart calmly looked at our staff after addressing his team in the locker room and said, "We might have gotten beat, but at least we paid for the volleyball program tonight." It was a light-hearted moment in the aftermath of a very disappointing loss.

The basketball drama continued into my junior year, which was the 1990-91 season. It began in October with a press conference to announce the sanctions placed on the program after the NCAA investigation. There sat the chancellor, the athletics director, and Norm Stewart at the microphone announcing that assistant coaches Bob Sundvold and Rich Daly would not have their contracts renewed following the season. We could not go to the 1991 NCAA Tournament. We lost scholarships. I remember watching Coach Stewart's wife, Virginia, shed tears during the press conference. It was difficult to watch and I'm sure embarrassing for all.

But we made the most of it. It was Doug Smith's senior season and Anthony Peeler was a junior. The two future NBA first round draft selections led us to another Big 8 Tournament championship with a 90-82 victory over Nebraska in the 1991 championship game. It was another pro-Missouri crowd at Kemper Arena that afternoon. We tore down the nets that day but had nowhere to go. This was our NCAA Tournament. It was bittersweet. Coach Daly ended up returning the next season as an assistant coach after winning an appeal on charges of unethical conduct with the NCAA. He remained on Coach Stewart's staff until he retired.

My senior year of 1991-92, the basketball team returned to the NCAA Tournament. It was Anthony Peeler's senior season. Of course, we needed about five hours, a tornado near the arena, and a power outage inside the arena to win our first-round game against West Virginia.

Looking back, it was a great thrill and a joy to be a tiny part of the overall athletics program at Mizzou, observing from a close distance as a student assistant writing a few press releases for the golf team and keeping stats for football, basketball, and baseball. As Coach Stewart might say, I'm sure that I looked like a frog in a hailstorm.

Today, it's a great joy to be in Columbia for a football game day. It's hard to believe how far that Gary Pinkel has brought the program in such a short time. The greatest week of my life came in November 2007, when Mizzou defeated Kansas at Arrowhead Stadium, won the Big 12 North title, and the top ranking in the national polls, and my first child was born 48 hours later.

Another symbol of the affection Mizzou fans have for the Jayhawks.
Photo courtesy of Daniel Turner

These Tigers are Fanatics

LARRY MOORE

Graduate of the University of Missouri School of Journalism and an award-winning anchorman for KMBC-TV in Kansas City

I can tell you one thing about Missouri football … it's a lot easier to be a part of a fundraising campaign when the team is winning. And we've certainly been winning lately. I am just so proud of the university and all it has accomplished. I believe that Coach (Gary) Pinkel is doing it the right way and look how Coach (Mike) Anderson is turning the basketball team around. Being a part of the Missouri family is something very, very special. You run into members of that family no matter where you are in the country – and when the teams are having success, you have a lot of great things to talk about. I have a friend out in Los Angeles and he'll call and ask me about Chase Daniel or Jeremy Maclin; those kids made an impact on people all over the country. It's just wonderful to see young men and women enjoy success like that while they are getting a wonderful education.

MARK PATEK

University of Missouri Class of 1987, a former football and baseball player who owns Tiger Town, a Missouri-themed retail store

When you play a sport, it stays in your blood forever. I think that's one reason I enjoy Tiger Town, because I get to be around great Missouri sports fans and we can talk Mizzou sports all we want – and it's part of my job! I played football one year and baseball four years, and played against Barry Bonds and Pete Incaviglia – who was the all-time NCAA single-season home run leader (48). I guess my real claim to fame from Missouri – although I didn't think it was any big deal at the time – was that I was Harry Caray's stepson's roommate. His name was Roger Johnson and we'd go down to Harry's home in Palm Springs. Harry knew everyone, and when he was down announcing baseball, he and his wife, "Dutchie," would go down and Roger and I would go down, too. We'd be out at the pool and Bob Hope or Frank Sinatra would walk in and start talking and drinking with Harry. I was a kid, so I didn't think anything about being with Sinatra or Bob Hope. "Dutchie" was like my second mom and they really made me feel at home. But I'd rather just swim in the pool than hang out with all the famous people who came to see Harry. It was just a part of a great time at Missouri. And now, with the way the football team has come back and guys like Chase (Daniel) and Chase (Coffman) and J-Mac (Jeremy Maclin) have made such big names for themselves, it's great to be able to talk Mizzou sports and have all the talk be so positive.

ROB FITZGERALD

Defensive back at the University of Missouri from 1974-77 who went on to enjoy fame as the Budweiser "I Love You, Man" actor

I played during a good time for Missouri football under Coach Al Onofrio. We beat some good teams those years, including Ohio State, Alabama, USC, and Nebraska. In fact we came back from a 21-6 halftime deficit at Ohio State to beat them on a two-point conversion. I remember because Woody Hayes blew his stack.

The camaraderie and brotherhood that developed between the players was unbelievable. Those ties have bound us throughout the years. The other day my mother pulled out pictures of me in my Mizzou uniform to show my 11-year-old son. The pride in her eyes brought back memories of how she and my father would jump in the Winnebago and follow the football team across the country to all the games. They always said those were the best times of their lives. The Southern Cal win was another game that I vividly remember. We are playing in California and I have a number of cousins that live out there that came to the game. I remember the (Los Angeles) Coliseum being electric, but the funniest thing was when I came off the field after a defensive stop and my uncle slapped me on the back and said, "Good job." It seems that he had snuck down onto the sidelines without the security guards noticing. This was something he was able to do quite often. It was great to have him on the sidelines, but then a security guard came by and asked if he was part of the team. Our equipment manager took one look at my uncle and then at me and then, to my surprise, told the guard that he was indeed part of the team. Later that year, he snuck down on the sideline towards the end of the Colorado game. I can still remember walking off the field talking to the Buffaloes and my uncle.

How many Kansas freshmen does it take to change a light bulb?

None. That's a sophomore course.

ROGER TWIBELL

Kansas City radio talk-show host and longtime network broadcaster

A number of years ago I was doing a golf event in Hawaii when I received a call from ABC asking me if I was interested in staying over a couple of extra days to broadcast the Rainbow Classic. I enjoyed doing men's college basketball, so I agreed to do the games.

Two questions I didn't ask were: Who was in the tournament, and who would be my analyst for the games? The first question was answered when I picked up the newspaper and saw that the first game would include Missouri. I have never had a problem doing a Missouri game even though I am a Kansas grad, but I knew that Coach Stewart might not be too happy to see me. Now I had about a day to figure out who was going to do the color with me.

The next morning I still had not found an adequate analyst. Basketball wasn't exactly king in Hawaii. Then it all seemed to come together for the broadcast. While walking down the beach I ran into Bud Stallworth (a former Kansas great). He was there on vacation. So I asked him if he would do the broadcast with me. He asked who was playing and I told him it was Missouri. He then asked if Coach Stewart would have a problem with us. I told him, "I hope not," with a little hesitation in my voice.

With about 10 minutes to go in warm-ups, Coach Stewart comes walking out of the locker room. As he passed us at the scorer's table, he did a double-take. When he realized that we were the broadcast team for the game, he gave us a look that would stop you in your tracks.

BILL KIRSHER

A 40-year University of Missouri Tigers fan

Over the years I have seen many exciting games and have heard some great Tiger Tales. There's one that I lived through, and another that I wish I had witnessed.

A dear friend of mine through my days at Mizzou was Coach Clay Cooper. He was a tremendous coach and an even better scout. He could pick up tendencies by the opposing team that most coaches could just dream about. No detail was too small for him to examine. I don't know how many wins it helped the football team garner, but I do know of one.

The first game I ever attended was against Kansas. They had an All-America named Charlie Hogue in the backfield. It was a cold day with the wind really blowing. As the game started, Coach Cooper noticed something very revealing about Hogue. Every time he was going to carry the ball, he licked his hands on the way up to the line of scrimmage. It was like a poker player giving away his hand. Coach Cooper quickly relayed this bit of information down to the field and alerted the rest of the coaching staff, who in turn told the defensive players to keep an eye on Hogue's hands and tongue.

Over and over, he licked his hands prior to a carry. And every time the Tigers keyed on it and were there to stop him for no gain. It worked and the Tigers came out the upset winner in that game.

> Why did Texas choose orange as their team color?
>
> You can wear it for the game on Saturday, hunting on Sunday, and picking up trash along the highways the rest of the week.

94

A few years later, I heard the story about two die-hard Tiger fans from Kansas City. One weekend, with the Tigers playing in Lincoln, they decided to take their wives with them to the game. In those days there was a train that went from Kansas City to Lincoln. They decided this would be the best way to get there so that they could start game preparations on the ride up to Nebraska.

When they got to the game they were well on their way to being insulated with drink. However, the day was bitter cold and at halftime they decided to go down beneath the stands to get out of the cold. Once down there they spotted a guy who looked like a janitor. They asked him if there was someplace they could go to get warm. He pointed to a door and said it was open and there were some chairs inside. They sat down to warm up and have a couple more drinks from their flask. As they heard the teams come back on the field, they got up and left the room. Once outside they saw the same man who had pointed them to the open room. They said they were much obliged and offered him a drink.

Unbeknownst to them, he was a policeman hired to make sure no one was drinking at the game. Knowing they were Tiger fans from the way they were dressed, he slapped the cuffs on them and took them to jail. When the game ended their wives went looking for them, but could not find them. After someone suggested they call the police station, they located them at the nearest precinct. Upon arriving to bail them out, the first question out of the "prisoners'" mouths was "Did we win?" Now that is a true Mizzou fan!

JEFF BARGE

Missouri football fanatic

I'll always remember 1997 as the year Mizzou football was relevant again. Columbia was buzzing about football for the first time in my memory, the mighty Huskers were in town, and I was lucky enough to have tickets. Our seats were on the students' side, about four rows up on the 50-yard line. I was front-and-center for the biggest Mizzou game of my life; when the Tigers scored on a long drive to start the game, I knew it was going to be special. To say the stadium was electric is an understatement. Mizzou was up by a touchdown at halftime and everyone in attendance was buzzed with the endorphins of being a contender.

The fourth quarter rolled around and I could hear the whispers that we were going to beat the best team in the nation. I've never been one to count my eggs before they've hatched. I can remember chiding, "Don't jinx us." My heart had been broken before; I didn't want to get my hopes up and drink the Kool-Aid. With a minute left, Mizzou up by seven, and Nebraska deep in their own territory, I finally conceded and said, "We're actually going to win this thing." I truly believed it; at that moment, the game was already won in my mind.

By this time, we could physically feel the push of students itching to storm the field. We didn't care, we made room. We were all reveling in this together.

The Cornhuskers started moving the ball as the seconds ticked off the clock. With seven seconds to go, (Nebraska quarterback Scott) Frost threw the ball into the end zone, it fell towards the ground, and was kicked into Husker hands. It was then that I felt the pang of impending doom.

The Flea Kicker.

The car was silent as we left Faurot Field. Nobody wanted to talk about it. We were beat up, completely exhausted, and our hopes were dashed.

I remember not wanting to do anything but go home and sleep, but we decided to get something to eat and dull the pain with a beer or six.

At the restaurant, there was almost as much Nebraska red as Mizzou black and gold. Everyone there looked spent; we had all been through the ringer. To their credit, I remember the almost apologetic nature of the Cornhusker fans, amazingly gracious in triumph. They admitted that they escaped Columbia by the skin of their teeth. One fan told me it was the greatest football game he'd ever seen. I'll agree, but with an exception – it was the greatest football game I've ever seen where I got my guts kicked out.

CHUCK EVERITT

President of the Missouri Tiger Club

I have been a Tiger fan all my adult life. I have been with Mizzou sports through the good times and the bad. From 1993-1999, I carried the cord for the coach's headset during the football games. Back in those days, the head coach didn't have wireless headsets.

I will never forget prior to my first game Coach Larry Smith's wife gave me a piece of advice. She told me never to turn my back on him because he turns quick and moves faster than he looks. I took this advice to heart and always kept an eye on Coach Smith.

One game however, I turned away when I heard a player yell. When I turned back it was too late. Coach Smith was on top of me and we hugged. It wasn't because he was happy to see me, but rather to keep us both from falling. I learned my lesson and never took my eyes off him again during a game.

Coach Smith was a very family-oriented man and his wife was very involved with the team. In fact, I can remember standing on the sideline, carrying the cord, when his wife came down and started pumping up the players. It must have worked because we beat Oklahoma State that day in four overtimes.

RAY PHILLIPS

University of Missouri alum and benefactor

I got involved with the athletic department when I was a student and I am still very much involved today. I started giving the university $50 a year – because that's all I could afford at the time. I've given a little more since then (over $350,000, including a $50,000 donation to help build the new assistant athletic director's office). I'm good friends with the chancellor, although I jokingly tell him that "this well is going to go dry someday" and I've visited with Coach (Gary) Pinkel. We talk about players and I enjoy visiting with the assistant coaches. I've been on the team plane and gone to Texas three times, Oklahoma three times, Nebraska and Colorado three times, and Baylor once. I'm going to Oklahoma State this year and I look forward to those trips.

Coach Pinkel (left) and Mr. Missouri, Ray Phillips.
Photo courtesy of Ray Phillips

We travel with the team, stay at the same hotel, go to the game on the same type of bus the team goes on – it's all first class. Until the NCAA made some rules changes, I was a volunteer who would look at young men in the area and talk with Coach Clay Cooper – one of the finest men I ever knew. If he asked for film I'd get it and send it to him. My last player was Andy Lock, who was a four-year guard (1986-89). Then, the NCAA told schools they couldn't have volunteers like me, so I was done. I miss it – but I still get out to area high schools. I don't go so much for the games; I like to go watch practices and see how the young men perform when no one's watching them. That's when you can tell a lot about a kid.

I have so many memories that I could never list them all. I guess No. 1 would be when we beat Alabama and Bear Bryant in the Gator Bowl. I remember going to basketball games at Brewer Fieldhouse. You'd hope that you could dodge the pigeons, because they were always in there and they – well, you know what pigeons do best – you just hoped they didn't do it on you!

A few years ago, I won the MU Alumni Association Tiger Pride Award and that was a great honor. But I don't do what

The Zou Crew, the Antlers, and other Missouri fans make life difficult for opposing teams.
Photo courtesy of Daniel Turner

I do for the honors or the recognition. I do it for the kids and for Missouri.

LARRY MOORE

Kansas City anchorman and University of Missouri alum and longtime friend of Ray Phillips

We don't call him Ray or Mr. Phillips. We just call him Mr. Missouri or Mr. Tiger, because Ray Phillips is the University of Missouri.

JUSTIN MOORE

University of Missouri sophomore

I've been a Mizzou fan since I knew what sports were. They were the team I first watched and I have always loved them. My family lives and dies with Missouri Tiger football.

You don't get better than Mizzou football. There's just nothing like it.

My favorite memory was when a bunch of my friends at Blue Springs South and Blue Springs decided we just weren't going to go to our (high school) Homecoming.

I think there were about 10 of us. We had been to all of our previous homecomings. Honestly, we knew this one wasn't going to be that great.

The guys and I had been talking about the Mizzou-Nebraska game coming up, and how awesome it would be to go. And it was actually my friend, Jordan, who suggested we go.

It didn't take a whole lot of time for us to say, "Oh yeah. We are definitely up for that."

We had to buy our tickets online. We would probably have ended up going to Homecoming if we had waited to buy them on game day. They actually ended up pretty much the same price per person as our Homecoming tickets, so it was a hell of a trade off, even with our seats on the grass.

We got (to Columbia) about 3 p.m. Kickoff wasn't for another five hours. So we walk down Ninth Street, visit The Artisan, a couple of Mizzou stores, and of course, Shakespeare's Pizza, which, of course, was packed. We didn't even bother ordering a pizza. It would be game time before we got it, anyway.

Parking was even more of a fiasco. I think we ended up parking a couple of miles away from Faurot Field. The throngs of people impeded every step. The smell of beer was everywhere you went. The place was just nuts.

And we never complained, because it was just too amazing to see. The M-I-Z-Z-O-U's were everywhere you went. We had to have said it no less than 500 times that day.

So two hours before kickoff, we grab our spot on the hill, right by the rock M, and just watch the teams warm up. A lot was riding on this game: A top 25 spot, supremacy in the Big 12 North, bragging rights. We just wanted to win it so badly.

We slaughter them. From the kick off to the final gun, it was flood gates wide open. The best part was, no one expected it. Not even the Tiger fans. The looks on the Cornhusker fans' faces were priceless. It was utter shock. The best part was when the whole stadium got the wave going, and when it got to the Nebraska section, it'd die for a second and everyone would boo them, and then they would just skip over them and start it back up.

The thing with Missouri is, it only gets better. That was my favorite memory of Mizzou, but I know that I'll have more favorite memories. It's unlike anything.

One thing I've realized with Missouri Tiger fans is how persistent they really are. If they want something, they're determined to get it. I'm honored to share this trait with my fellow black-and-gold bleeders.

JUNLONG LI

University of Missouri graduate student and teaching assistant

I'm a graduate student and teaching assistant, majoring and specializing in statistics, at the University of Missouri. I came over from China three years ago to MU.

When I think of Missouri sports, I think of football. There's just nothing like it. When I first saw it, I was blown away. It's just power. That's it. I mean in soccer and basketball, it requires skill and speed, but football, you do everything. You need to pass, catch, kick, and run. You need everything.

I think football is the sport of men. You're just trying to push over the guy in front of you.

When I first watched, I had no idea what the rules were, so I had to go with my friends and have them explain to me everything – touchdowns, field goals, interceptions, fumbles, all of that. But once I learned the rules, I fell in love with the sport.

I played it a little bit on Stankowski Field with my friends and other people and played in the flag football league. I think my favorite position was kicker. I always wanted to be a kicker. But it's hard to be kicker. Kicking a soccer ball is so much easier than kicking a football. It's a big difference.

My favorite player last year was Jeff Wolfert. He was the perfect kicker. He never missed. He hit every extra point he attempted in his college career. I saw him kick a field goal over 40 yards and it blew me away. How do you do that?! It was awesome to see.

I really enjoy the circumstances and the environment with Mizzou football. It's just crazy. People yelling and screaming their heads off. You just can't stop feeling how awesome it is. It's really quite amazing to see.

What really blew me away were the people. I kind of knew the history after researching a little bit and people just telling me, but I didn't know how important it was to the people and the fans. My first game was two years ago against Illinois and we had to drive to St. Louis to watch the game. I was just like, "You people are crazy."

But the Nebraska game two years ago was unbelievable. Just unbelievable. There were so many people driving up from the north, from the south, everywhere. The streets were just lined with cars. You couldn't park anywhere. The place was swarming with Missouri fans. I was extremely impressed.

That game, we killed them. It was by far my favorite game. The NBA and college basketball is awesome to me, but football was my favorite sport after that game. It's my favorite sport to watch and play. I'm really excited to watch this year and the years to come.

DARRIN "TRUMAN THE TIGER" WIDDICK

University of Missouri, Class of 1989 and a former Truman the Tiger

When I went to Missouri, I had no intention of trying out for the Truman the Tiger mascot position. But I read about the tryouts in the student newspaper and decided to go see what they were all about with a buddy of mine. Truman the Tiger, who is named after (former President) Harry Truman, had been introduced right around the time I enrolled at Missouri and everyone was really excited about the new mascot. My buddy, Mike Hill, had played football in high school, and he was looking into the cheerleader tryouts. I talked to the cheerleading and spirit coach, and thought, what the heck, I'd try out for Truman. I got the big tiger head on, got into the body suit, and put on the gloves. They had us sing the school fight song and perform a song of our choice. There were no real guidelines. So I performed in front of a panel of judges – ironically, I later became one of those judges – and I got the job. I was one of four or five individuals who performed as Truman. Back then, I worked with Joe Castiglione, who was the director of marketing. Joe was a great guy and eventually became the MU athletic director. I worked with him as an intern and really enjoyed my association with him.

In the beginning, much of Truman's routine was ad-libbed and unstructured. He was brand new and the fans loved him. Like I said, we had four or five different "Trumans," but we had just one costume, so we'd always try to take it home and wash it to help the next guy out. People would ask what it was like to perform as Truman at the early-season games when it was really hot. And to tell you the truth, the heat never bothered me. I was an 18- or 19-year-old kid and I was doing what I loved. I lost a few pounds at some games, but I never even thought about the heat. Although I remember one spring football game when it was 87 or 88 degrees and I couldn't keep the sweat out of my eyes. If the fans wondered why Truman kept running into a little shed that day, it was to take off the head and wipe the sweat from my eyes because I couldn't see anything. On the other hand, one year I traveled to Colorado for a football game and I can assure you that I was the warmest person on the field that day.

A year after I graduated, I called the university and told the people who worked with Truman that I had a special night planned and I was wondering if they could help me. I wanted Truman to help me propose to my wife. I purchased a roll of newsprint and made this sign that ran from mid-court to the baseline of the Missouri basketball court that read: "Susan: Marry Me?" Susan was an MU student who was going to dental school in Kansas City and we decided to go see a basketball game together. She was a big sports fan and was real excited about going to the game. A friend of mine came over to my parents' house to help me paint the sign; Susan drove by and called. She saw my friend's car and asked if she could come over, too. I told her we were working on something and I think she was mad that we didn't invite her over. Well, we finally went to the game

> Hey! I hear KU's a four-year school now!

and we smuggled in the sign. She never did see it and had no idea what was going to happen at halftime. At the half, I asked her to go down to the court, because we were in nosebleed seats. She said, "We can't go down on the court." I got her to go down and that's when Truman and the cheerleaders unrolled the sign. The Antlers started chanting: "Just say no!" Another group started to chant:

> **"We had four or five different "Trumans," but we had just one costume, so we'd always try to take it home and wash it to help the next guy out. "**

"Marry the bum!" She didn't know what to think. She never really did say yes that night, but she wound up marrying me and I guess you could say I have Truman the Tiger to thank for that.

Dr. MARK MANCIN

Devious dentist and longtime Missouri fan

I've told this story numerous times over the last few years and everyone seems to get a nice chuckle. It is called "The KU Crown Caper."

One day in my dental practice, I had a patient request a special crown made with the KC Chiefs logo on it. He was a die-hard fan and was in need of a crown so he thought this would be a great way to show his fan loyalty. He had contemplated a tattoo but this seemed much easier. Well, in the chair next to this patient was one of my rabid, die-hard Jayhawk fans. This guy was Mr. KU. He was very full of himself and his beloved Kansas University. Ironically, he never attended KU – which seems to be quite common.

Anyway, he overheard my conversation and it just so happened he was scheduled to have a crown done on this particular day. He was as excited as a little boy at Christmas time and I was becoming ill with the mere thought of having to handle the (situation) with my highly trained and skilled hands. Then it struck me. This was my opportunity to get even. To settle a score that was long overdue.

You see, this guy was constantly badgering and harassing me when it came to the MU-KU rivalry. Every time he came for his dental appointment, he would do some mischievous act that revolved around KU and that miserable bird. He would hang banners in my waiting room; put little KU Jayhawk stickers all over the mirrors in the patient bathroom; text me on my cell phone whenever they won a game; and send me photos of the "bird." Then one day he went too far. He placed little bird decals on my truck windows and bumper and covered up my MU decals with KU crap. These actions put me over the threshold. You don't mess with my truck and you don't defame the Missouri flag and banner.

For years I have tolerated endless grief from this beaker and now the golden opportunity presented itself. Being the consummate salesperson, I went out of my way to show him some samples of the crowns with logos on them. I even got on the phone with the laboratory that makes the crown and went over all options in detail. He was quite taken aback that I was willing to go the extra mile for him ... especially since the topic was KU related. No problem, I told him. The minute he finalized his decision, we initiated treatment.

After he was numbed with local anesthetic, the tooth was prepared for the crown, an impression was taken, and the lab was contacted. I told them the patient wanted a KU logo on his crown, but I also instructed them to make a second crown with the MU Tiger logo on it. The lab technician – also a loyal foot soldier of MU – began to chuckle: "You're not going to do what I thing you're doing?" "Oh, yes, I am."

The patient was placed in a temporary crown and I kicked his (rear-end) out the door. Just kidding.

Two weeks later, he returned for his precious little bird crown. With the skill of a magician, I showed him his KU crown and then masterfully replaced it with the MU Tiger crown. The crown was cemented. Now came the tricky part. We had to distract him and provide confidence that all was well with his new bird crown. While we were trying the crown in, we snuck a couple of photographs of the crown in place. After we cemented the MU crown, we pretended to take a picture with the camera again but of course we had already taken the picture of the KU crown. We popped the pic up on the computer screen and told him how wonderful it looked and gave him a big hug – NOT! We did print a picture of the crown so the proud parent could show all of his KU brethren his supposedly spanking new KU crown. When he went to the front desk, he immediately sticks two fingers in his mouth and retracts his cheek to show the girls at the front desk his new crown. The girls comment on how cool it was but he might be better off showing the photograph to people because it was impossible to see that far back in his mouth (nice cover-up by the girls ... well trained in espionage). Now we just sit back and wait to see how long it takes for him to realize he does not have a KU crown but rather he is sporting the MU Tiger logo.

> **❝ With the skill of a magician, I showed him his KU crown and then masterfully replaced it with the MU Tiger crown. ❞**

Two weeks later I get a phone call from my KU patient and boy is he hacked off! He called me every name in the book and some I can never begin to repeat. He busted my chops up one side and down the other. Finally, he ran out of oxygen and then I asked him, "How does it feel?" He replied, "The crown feels great, but I do not appreciate your sense of humor!" I said, "Ditto! After all these years of your harassment and egomaniacal comments about your beloved Jayhawks and poor jokes and jabs about my Tigers, I can finally say I got even."

He says, "What I did is nothing compared to what you did! You have physically and emotionally scarred me for life!"

Say what? I'm now getting a bad sense about what I had done. Mr. KU jokester is hinting legal action...scarred for life ... emotional and physical trauma. I can see me appearing on the "People's Court" TV program. I hear the music playing ... "And now the case of an emotionally distraught KU fan vs. the psychotic MU dentist ... Let's hear what Judge Wapner has to say ... "

Fortunately for me, it never materialized into legal action nor did he file a complaint against me with the Missouri Dental Board, even though he mentioned it to me. I laughed when he brought it up and actually told him the Missouri Dental Board would probably laugh hysterically when he told them the story. I had to remind him you are a Kansas guy trying to convince a bunch of Missouri dentists (of which

> GOD
> I HATE
> KU
>
> *May their cars crash into*
> *the Missouri River,*
>
> *May they die a fiery death,*
>
> *And may the catfish gnaw*
> *On their charred bones.*

A touching tribute to Mizzou's hated rival.
Photo courtesy of Mark Vickery

90 percent are graduates of MU and UMKC) to punish a dentist from Missouri because he pulled a prank on a KU guy ... Hmmm! What would I do if I was on the board?

Anyway, the story finally comes to closure when I removed the MU crown and placed the KU one. He actually had a witness observe to verify the KU crown was cemented in his mouth. My staff found it quite humorous. Needless to say, he left my practice a year later when he found a KU grad who was granted a DDS by UMKC, which is part of the University of Missouri school system. You can run but you can't hide.

GREG HALL

Kansas City's social commentator and Nebraska fan

I don't know how many stories in this book will be contributed by Nebraska fans, but here is one.

I graduated the year before I witnessed the greatest college football game I have ever had the privilege of viewing with my own eyes. The year was 1978 and my Cornhuskers had just defeated the legendary Billy Sims and the Oklahoma Sooners in the greatest Nebraska win since

Bob Devaney's back-to-back National Championships in 1970 and 1971.

Tom Osborne had carried the weight of losing to Barry Switzer and his Sooners at the end of every Big 8 season for five consecutive years. Whispers were becoming catcalls as Husker Nation began to question whether or not Dr. Tom would ever slay the crimson giant from the south. But a Billy Sims fumble late in the game sealed the conference title, an Orange Bowl bid, and the nation's No. 1 ranking for Nebraska. All that was left was a little game against the Missouri Tigers in Lincoln the following Saturday. It was nothing more than a quirk in the schedule that had the Huskers close with the Tigers, rather than the Sooners, that year.

Missouri was led by Warren Powers and the Tigers were closing out a winning, but disappointing season. This was in the day when six wins meant you were embarrassed, not heading to some toilet bowl. The Tigers had dropped two of their last three games heading into Lincoln and were staring at finishing 6-5 with another loss to the Big Red. This game was merely a tune-up for the Huskers, who would be accepting a bid to the Orange Bowl following the game. The only real mystery of the day is who the Orange Bowl committee would pair the 10-0 Huskers against.

I started sneaking into (Nebraska's) Memorial Stadium in high school. It became somewhat of a learned art form. No stadium, arena, and possibly even a few county jails are guarded as well as the walls that house Nebraska football. Being one of 15 children, I was quick to experiment with and learn alternative methods of gaining entry into sporting events other than with the typical paid-for ticket.

Early in the season, my Omaha friends and I would drive down to Lincoln before dawn and scale the cyclone fencing at the most vulnerable corner of the stadium. We would then hide in the upper regions of the concrete mass perched behind one of the many stone exits. As the season lengthened, the weather became too frigid for this maneuver.

The Missouri game was held in late November and winter was already starting to descend on the Nebraska prairie. Our alternative plan of entry was a deal we had struck with some of the Nebraska gymnasts. They performed flips and acrobatics on the sidelines during the game and were all given color-coded ribbons for each game to allow them to enter at no charge. For $5 these gymnasts would slip us their ribbon through the fence and we would enter unchallenged.

I mention this because it quickly led me to attempt even bolder acts to gain access to forbidden places. On a trip to Kansas City one summer, I took my camera down to the infield of Royals Stadium and managed to sit in the third-base photographer's booth for a game against Reggie Jackson and the Yankees. The photog's bay was adjacent to the Yankee dugout. My elbow rested on the same iron bar as Yogi Berra's.

My roommate and I sat courtside at Allen Fieldhouse in 1979 when Larry Bird's Indiana State Sycamores battled Sidney Moncrief's Arkansas Razorbacks in the NCAA tourney that year. I still have a photo I snapped

What does the "N" on Nebraska's football helmets stand for?

"Nowledge."

of my roomie standing next to a startled Bird during their warm-up drills. We got there simply by acting like we belonged.

I used the same brashness to gain entrance into Missouri's locker room that November afternoon inside Memorial Stadium. I used my camera to make me look official and a brisk walk to avoid any examinations.

Once inside it was easy. The players were quietly preparing for the game but they all enjoyed the attention from a photographer. For all they knew I was a fresh young *Sports Illustrated* photog who was there to capture the game for the magazine. They had no idea I was a Nebraska fan simply in awe of the spectacle known as college football.

Kellen Winslow posed for me by holding his helmet off to his right side, like you would envision in a yearbook photo. Phil Bradley was not in the picture-taking mood as he sat folding and unfolding his hands. The locker room was cramped and Warren Powers, Mizzou's head coach, was nowhere to be found. That may be why so many of the players were happy to pose for my camera.

Powers finally did appear from the back of the locker room but never spoke a word. The room fell coffin silent as he made his way past the players. A school-room blackboard on wheels sat in the center of the locker room. Without mouthing a word, Powers moved toward the board and picked up a stubby piece of chalk.

With his back to his team, he scratched out the following sentence in large, deliberate capital letters. "LET'S F#*K 'EM UP!" As Powers dotted the exclamation point of his message, the sound from the Missouri athletes jammed into that south end-zone locker room exploded like a war had broken out. The team nearly ripped the double doors from their hinges as they shot onto the field and ran toward the sidelines.

What followed was the greatest game I ever saw. Nebraska was magnificent. Missouri was simply better. James Wilder wrote himself into the soul of every Nebraska fan who watched him play that day. He literally assaulted the Nebraska defense run after run after run.

I walked back to my car, listening to the post-game show on my transistor radio. I remember thinking how lucky I was to have witnessed such an incredible football game. My heart was broken that my Huskers had lost and that their undefeated season was now dust. But the game was such an epic battle that I thought it fitting to lose yet be proud.

The radio announced that the Orange Bowl Committee had just invited Tom Osborne and his Huskers to play in Miami on January 1st. Their opponent? A rematch with the Oklahoma Sooners. I cursed loudly as I started the car's engine.

MARILYN ROSE THUDIUM

aka "The Flag Lady"

When I was a little girl, my father was a postmaster and he used to close up early on Saturday and we would grab the lunch that my mother would pack and head to the Mizzou football games. That was over 70 years ago. Over the years, I have become know as the "Flag Lady" and house mom for the Alpha Chi Omega sorority.

Marilyn Rose Thudium – the Flag Lady – has become a fixture on Aisle 39 at Faurot Field.
Photo courtesy of Jen Stipetich

Growing up a Tiger fan was wonderful and when my future husband received a football scholarship to play for them, I was ecstatic. However, due to the war he never got the chance to don a Tiger uniform. And when he came back we purchased our first set of season tickets in 1948. The ticket package back then was $50. I am not sure but I might be the longest tenured season ticket holder. Nothing can keep me from going to a Tiger football game. In fact, five days after I gave birth to my daughter, I was seated in my seats off Aisle 39.

My reign as the flag lady started in 1978. We loaded up a Winnebago and headed to the Nebraska game in Lincoln.

Prior to the game I had made a black and gold flag that I intended to wave at the game on a pole I had rigged up. Somehow I convinced the ushers to let me down on the field (I think it was because I sang the national anthem so eloquently.) I actually led the team on the field waving my flag. Not bad for a lady in her 50s.

Since that day, I have brought my flag and waved it while running up and down aisle 39 after every touchdown. However, after (the 9-11 terrorist tragedies) they put in a new rule that poles were not allowed in the stadium. For awhile, I just waved my flag, but it wasn't the same. Then, after I had surgery, I walked with the aid of a cane for a while. At one game I decided to slip the flag on the cane so I could wave it better and it worked. I still bring my cane to games, but only to use as my flag holder. Even the director of athletics has helped me live my passion for Mizzou football. At one game a security guard came up to me and said that I couldn't use my cane to wave the flag. However, a couple of days later I ran into Mike Alden and explained the situation. He told me not to worry about it and I haven't seen that security guard since.

The last couple of years my kids have sent me to the bowl games as a Christmas present. They were some of the best gifts I have ever received. Oh, and by the way, for Kansas games I add a plucked chicken to the top of the flag.

So, if you are ever at a Tiger football game, look up to Aisle 39 after we score a touchdown and I will be the older woman running back and forth with the flag.

JOE ZWELLINGER

Missouri grad and owner of the Westport Flea Market

As a member of the Zeta Beta Tau fraternity, we were very active in following our teams at Mizzou. In order to get the best seats at basketball games, I would bribe one of the ticket interns to ensure we were in the top five of the lottery every year. Consequently, our seats were always front-and-center next to the Antlers. By the fourth year when Coach Stewart would bring out doughnuts for the students camping out for tickets (a Stewart tradition), he looked at me and just laughed because he knew no one's luck was that good. All I could do was wink and tell him not to worry. We would be there to yell our heads off.

My most memorable moment was during the NCAA tournament in California against Arizona. I am at the game and the PA announcer is just going nuts every time Arizona scores and barely says anything when we score. Finally, I had had enough. I went down to the scorer's table and started yelling at him that this wasn't a PAC-10 game and to be impartial. Security came and took me out of the arena. As I was being taken out, I could hear Al McGuire (who was doing the game on TV) tell the security guard that I was a "foxhole guy." I was told later that he mentioned the incident on TV and he said that I was right, that the announcer was being biased. I felt justified and left with a smile on my face. One thing that stuck with me was that he said I was a "foxhole guy." I didn't really understand it at the time, but later figured it out that he meant I would be a good guy to have in the foxhole with him. I guess that is what you can

Joe Zwellinger's sign about honking nearly drove his pregnant wife crazy.
Photo courtesy of Rich Zvosec

say about all Mizzou fans. We are "foxhole guys" because we stick up for our team, no matter what.

Since graduating, I have enjoyed following the teams and tweaking my Kansas neighbors. With football's recent success, I have always put signs in my front yard to support the Tigers. However, one time it back-fired on me. I put a sign up during the week leading up to Armageddon: Battle of KU and MU football in 1997. One said "Honk for MU." The other said "Beat KU." People started honking so much you would have thought it was a parade route. My wife, who was nine months pregnant at the time, was not too happy. Following the game, I went down to *The Kansas City Star* and bought 400 copies of the newspaper and spent all day pasting the newspapers on the windows of my KU friends and neighbors.

MIKE BRAUDE

University of Missouri Class of 1957, and former president of the Kansas City Board of Trade

I have had three loves in my life: my family, Mizzou sports, and the Board of Trade. I had two requirements for my sons when they got married: Marry someone from the opposite sex, and it had better not be a Jayhawk.

In my four years at Mizzou, I went to every home football, basketball, and baseball game. I will always remember when Coach Sparky Stallcup would come out and lead the band. One time when we had a fraternity formal dance scheduled the night of a game, I had a big decision to make. Should I skip the game? However, if I did, I would be fined $50. I decided my best option was to go to the game in my tux (so I could go straight to the dance). The only problem was that the game was going bad; our starting center fouled out and then his back-up did, as well. I didn't want to go to the dance in a bad mood, but then the third-string center, Arnie Koester, tipped in a missed shot for the win in overtime. I went to the dance a little late, but in a good mood.

My love for Mizzou sports got me through graduate school. After Mizzou I was scheduled to go to Columbia University for graduate school, but when I got there I was told I needed to take six more hours or take a proficiency exam to be exempted. Knowing that I was in trouble with those two options, I was told that the head of the department, Professor Edwards, could waive the credits. I was also told that he never does that, but I thought "what the heck?"

When I went to see him, I noticed two certificates hanging on his office wall from the University of Nebraska. So I asked him if he was a Cornhusker football fan. When he told me that he was, I decided to go for it. We had an hour-long conversation about Big 8 football that included me giving him the play-by-play of the Nebraska-Mizzou football game from the previous fall. At the end of the conversation, he called his secretary and told her to waive the six credits. Thank goodness for Tiger football.

Another time I went to the MU basketball game at Kansas and as I was sitting there Tom Watson came onto the court to present Coach Roy Williams the ball. Incensed that Watson was a Kansas City guy and a graduate of Stanford, I yelled out, "I should have rooted for England in the Ryder Cup." Coach Stewart never let me forget that.

> A Jayhawk was at a soda machine at the casino. A Tiger was next in line. The Jayhawk put in a dollar and bought a bottle of water. Then, she put in another dollar and received a bottle of lemon-ade. On the third time, the Tiger fan asked, "Are you done yet?" And the Jayhawk fan said, "Duh! No! I'm still winning!"

STEVE LAMPONE

Kansas City Parks and Recreation Department

I spent my formative years in Columbia and developed a true love for the Tigers during those days. As a 12-year-old, I would ride my bike across campus to the football games and sneak into the stadium. I would grab a program and get

Steve Lampone passes his love of the Tigers down through the generations.
Photo courtesy of Steve Lampone

as close to the field as possible. In those days, I could tell you every stat about each and every player.

I have passed on this love for the Tigers to my son and grandson. My son would go to every football game with me, including the tailgating festivities each morning of game day. In fact, even though my son attends K-State, he is still a diehard Tiger. His car has been keyed three times because he refuses to take off the MU sticker when he drives around the K-State campus.

So when my daughter had Gabe (my grandson), it was only natural that I would help him become a Tiger fan. He was born on October 13, 2007, the day of the heartbreaking loss to Oklahoma. I remember watching the game in the hospital waiting room. From the first day he came home, I would play the Mizzou fight song every morning. It really seemed to have a calming effect on him. His favorite book is Truman the Tiger and he can spot an MU logo on everything.

However, the most amazing thing is that at 21 months old, he has developed the habit of anytime he comes to the house he grabs the remote and wants the 2007 Highlights DVD of MU football turned on. After studying it, he grabs a football and starts to run around the house, imitating what he saw on the screen. He even hunches his shoulders like he is wearing shoulder pads. We have taken him along to Fan Appreciation Day and the Spring Game and he will soon attend his first real game.

It is a great feeling to share your love of MU sports with your son and grandson.

TOM BECKER

*Attended the University of Missouri Law School in the
1970s*

I have been a lifelong Tiger fan since my father used to take me to at least one football game each year. And even though I didn't go to Missouri for undergraduate school, I made up for it by going to MU Law School in the 1970s.

I always try to catch every game either in person or on TV/radio. A couple of years ago, my wife and I were planning a family vacation over Christmas and we scheduled it so we would be back in time for all of the BCS bowl games. Unfortunately, that year Missouri was relegated to the Alamo Bowl and I was sent looking for a place to watch the game in a foreign land.

The night of the game we were still in Buenos Aires on our family vacation, but I was determined that I was not going to miss this game. I know my wife thought I was off my rocker as I searched frantically on the Internet for a place to watch the game. As fate would have it, I stumbled across a bar called "El Alamo" that proudly said it had ESPN. I called and they assured me that the game would be on in their place.

When my wife and I arrived, the only thing on TV was the World's Strongest Man competition. After trying to explain to the bartender in English (I didn't speak Spanish) that I wanted one of the televisions to be changed to the Missouri game, he brought a TV behind the bar and worked on it until it somehow had a picture of the Alamo Bowl. The good news was I could watch the game. The bad news was that there was no sound. I didn't care as the Tigers jumped to an early lead and seemed to have the game in hand.

Then with West Virginia catching up, a fight started in the bar. And although I was knocked down once (accidentally), I continued to watch the game. It was like a scene out of a movie when everyone in the bar is fighting except for one guy. I am just glad that the Tigers held on and I could go back to the hotel with a smile on my face.

When I got back to the hotel my wife was asleep (she had left at halftime) and I had no one to celebrate with. However, I felt it was all worth it to see my Tigers get a bowl win.

> **" A fight started in the bar. And although I was knocked down once (accidentally), I continued to watch the game. It was like a scene out of a movie when everyone in the bar is fighting except for one guy. "**

BILL ROSS

Former longtime basketball coach at the University of Missouri-Kansas City

I was a senior at Paseo High School in Kansas City and I was being recruited by both Kansas and Missouri. Coach Phog Allen of KU had me over to Lawrence for a visit and I had almost decided to go to Kansas when my father got a call from a couple of local businessmen. The next week, I sat down with Dutton Brookfield and Vic Swyden, two very prominent Kansas Citians at the time.

They asked me a series of questions. It went something like this.

"Son, where do you live?" they asked.

My response was Kansas City.

"Son, what state is that in?"

My response was Missouri.

"Son, where is your high school located?"

My response was Kansas City.

"And what state is that high school in?"

Missouri.

"What state is your grade school in?"

Missouri.

"What state is your junior high in?"

Missouri.

"So what state have you represented?"

Missouri.

Finally, they asked, "What state do you think you should represent in college?"

My response was Missouri.

That is how I ended up at Missouri. Our coach was Sparky Stallcup and the best player on the team was Norm Stewart. He was a tremendous scorer. I can remember Coach Stallcup always telling me to get the ball to Norm and go down by the basket just in case he missed.

I am proud to say that I never lost to Kansas until my senior year.

BOB BABCOCK

Missouri alum and owner of Harpo's in Kansas City

One of my fondest memories of Mizzou football is when I was a freshman. It was an unwritten rule in my fraternity that you gave your tickets to an upperclassman when you were a freshman. If you didn't and went to the game using the tickets, you would be picked up and passed all the way up to the top of the stadium seating. I must admit it was a great ride, even though I ended up with a terrible seat.

BRETT LEWIS

1974 University of Missouri graduate, office managing partner of Grant Thornton LLP

I graduated from Mizzou in 1984. Since that time, our family has had season tickets, except for a period when we lived in Dallas and Denver. Needless to say, our three kids have grown up to be diehard Mizzou fans. During her grade school years in Denver, Hannah, who is our youngest and now 16, had a spelling test over the 50 states. Hannah was upset when my wife picked her up from school that day – she had missed one on the test. She looked up with a little smile even though the tears were welling in her eyes – she had missed "Missouri," spelling it "Mizzou."

> **"Hannah was upset when my wife picked her up from school that day – she had missed one on the test. She looked up with a little smile even though the tears were welling in her eyes – she had missed 'Missouri,' spelling it 'Mizzou.'"**

DOUG BATES

University of Missouri, Class of 1999

My sister and I are fifth-generation Mizzou grads, so our black-and-gold bloodlines and our hatred for our feathered neighbors to the west run deep. About 10 years ago, I was riding with my dad and grandparents to Lawrence to watch my brother's high school football game. My grandpa was beginning to struggle with his memory, and we have since learned that it was likely the early stages of Alzheimer's. But on this night, he would prove to be particularly lucid. So, as we drove into Lawrence on K-10, we passed the old Haskell Indian Football Stadium. When Granddad spotted it, he got immediately animated and aggravated. "That's Haskell Stadium!" he exclaimed. "We played Lawrence High there (he went to North Kansas City) during my senior year in 1939, and we got robbed on a pass interference call against me in the end zone late in the game! They went on to win and that terrible call was what cost us the game! And do you know who the referee was that threw the flag? It was Phog Allen."

KELLY RAY

Shelbyville, Missouri, resident and "famous lawn mower"

There's a big sign in the middle of town that says, "WELCOME TO SHELBYVILLE, THE HOME OF NORM STEWART, THE BASKETBALL COACH OF THE UNIVERSITY OF MISSOURI." We're all proud of Norm and proud that we're from Shelbyville. When I was a kid, I mowed Norm's dad's grass. Ken Stewart didn't like our mower, so I always mowed with his mower – a big John

Deere rider. As I'd mow, he'd sit in his garage and watch me. He was a carbon copy of Norm – a great guy, but he was a perfectionist. I never mowed his yard without him taking me out and showing me a place or two I could have done a better job. He liked it mowed on Fridays so "it would look good over the weekend." When I was done, he'd give me $20 and say, "You tell your dad I paid you $10." He told me that every time. And when I was done mowing, I knew that it was going to take about 20 to 30 minutes for Ken to tell me how to mow the yard. Sometimes, he just wanted to talk and I loved talking with him. Heck, I was just a kid and he was someone who could teach you a thing or two, if you paid attention. But you knew to add 20 to 30 minutes onto the end of how long it took to mow the yard because Ken was going to have something to say. He was something else. And so was Norm. In Shelbyville, there are so many Norm stories – he was your normal, ornery high school kid who loved to pull pranks. But he was also a great baseball and basketball player. When he went to MU, he made the entire community proud. In Shelbyville, everyone knew everyone else, so when Norm began coaching at Missouri, all the guys in town, including my dad and Ken Stewart, all went to the town coffee shop the next day to find out what Norm did right and the players did wrong. The coffee shop changed owners over the years so many times I don't really recall its name – I just know that when you went in the morning following a game, Ken Stewart was holding court and every guy in town was listening until he had to go to work.

As Ken got older, we would take him to watch Norm's basketball games at MU. We had a routine. Well, maybe I should say that Ken had a routine and we followed it. We always had to stop at this truck stop in Collier Junction, which is north of Columbia, so Ken could get something to eat. He loved that truck stop as much as he loved MU basketball. My dad would drive up to Hearnes and let my mom and Ken out of the car and Ken eventually had to sit in the handicapped seats and Norm let my mom and dad sit in his seats. They had those seats until Norm left the university. It was a great time to be an MU fan. When Norm came back to Shelbyville to see his dad or his friends, everyone turned out to see him. It was a great place to be a kid.

BRYAN PRATT

University of Missouri Class of 1995, law school 1999, and a state representative from Jackson County, Missouri.

The family of Missouri football fans is remarkable. I can go to a function and for one night, they don't care if I am a Republican, or a lawyer, or from a certain walk of life – I'm a Tiger. And that's what I love about the University of Missouri. There's a publisher who disagrees with everything I say or do, but that publisher is also from MU and if we're at a Missouri function, all we are is Tigers. We're part of that special Tiger family. If I go to a Missouri event, and see a lawyer who's on the other side of a case, it doesn't matter because he or she might be from Missouri, and on that night we're Tigers. I know that's hard to understand, unless you've experienced it.

I have so many wonderful memories of Missouri and the football games, even though we weren't as good back when I was in school as we are today. Back then, we had a great tradition. After Mizzou would score its first touchdown at

Maybe one day, from left, Cameron Woods, Mackenzie Hoffman, Aaron Hoffman, Carter Woods, Canton Woods and Jake Hoffman will help carry a goal post from Faurot Field to their favorite place in Columbia, Harpo's.
Photo courtesy of Rich Zvosec

home, we'd throw oranges out onto the field because the winner of the Big 8 got to go to the Orange Bowl. We never went when I was there, but I did happen to throw an orange and hit a future NFL player – Charlie Batch. He was playing for Eastern Michigan. Sorry about that, Charlie.

The greatest tradition at the University of Missouri was taking down the goal posts and walking to Harpo's following a big win. We'd take our own saw so we could cut off a piece of the goal post to keep for a souvenir. We finally got smart

> **" Tyus Edney – I don't think any of us will ever forget that one. "**

and one of us would park our car at Harpo's the night before, keep the saw in the trunk, and be ready – just in case it happened.

While the memories of my time at MU are priceless, there were a few that still sting. I remember sitting around a small TV, watching Missouri play UCLA in the NCAA basketball tournament. There were a few seconds left in the game and we're all high-fiving each other because Missouri was going to the Final Four. Then, Tyus Edney. Need I say more? Four second left – *four seconds* – and he drives the length of the court and hits the game-winning basket. We went from high-fives and celebrations to dead silence. That was the worst, the absolute worst moment, because we were so close to doing something no Missouri basketball team had ever done. There was the fifth-down game against Colorado and the "flea kicker" against Nebraska, but Tyus Edney – I don't think any of us will ever forget that one.

But those losses just made all the wins that much more special. The football team and basketball teams are making great strides. We have so many young men and women involved in Missouri sports we are proud of. It's just great to be a Tiger.

MARK NEWCOMER

University of Missouri, Class of 2002

I grew up playing football, basketball, and baseball. I could have gone to a small school and played one of those sports, but the only school I ever dreamed about going to was

Missouri. I played intramural sports at MU and had a great time. I wouldn't trade my MU experience for anything. I remember watching Doug Smith play basketball when I was a kid, and thinking, "That's where I'm going to school." I have so many memories that it could fill an entire book.

But one of my favorites happened my freshman year. It was the "flea kicker" game against Nebraska. We didn't win that game, but I remember seeing 25,000 Nebraska fans wearing their red shirts and I wondered if it would ever change. The great part of that story is when you fast-forward to 2007 and we beat Nebraska and all you see is black and gold. There couldn't have been more than 2,000 to 3,000 Nebraska fans at the game and I remember feeling so proud – thinking back to my freshman year, it seemed like there were more Nebraska fans at our games than MU fans. But even though we weren't as good when I was a student, nothing topped game day at Columbia.

My friends, about 20 of us, would tailgate about three hours before the game started. We had our same spot every game and made a day out of it. Now that we're all older, married and have kids, it's not quite what it used to be. But the games are so great it doesn't really matter. Now, we have the Tiger Walk, and that wasn't a part of Missouri football when I was a student. It's become a great tradition that all the fans get into. I think it really pumps up the players as much as it pumps up the fans.

But you know what it really means to be a Missouri football fan? Standing in line for about three hours to get a photo of Chase Daniel with my son, Mack. Mack's so young that he won't remember this, but I'll have that picture forever. I sent it to all my MU friends – and even a few KU fans, too. I haven't made it into a poster, but I'm trying to talk my wife into making it into a Christmas card.

FRED ROSSLAN

President of Pro Stone LLC and the originator of the Tiger toilet

I guess you could call me a dreamer. Like it says on my business card: If you can dream it, we can build it. We do bathroom renovation and custom concrete floor and shower work. We were working on a big project and everything was being done in MU colors and I was asked about creating an MU toilet. I experimented with some different paints that would stick to porcelain and I came up with the Tiger toilet. I got some old toilets and practiced on them and now, we offer the Tiger toilet, and no two are alike because each one is hand painted. We're licensed with the university and right now have about 75 of them – some have been delivered and some are still in the shop. Each one takes about three to four hours to paint and we coat them with a clear coat so the paint won't rub off.

Some folks heard about the toilets and I got a call from the Children's Miracle Network. They wanted something special for a telethon and I painted a toilet and took it to the MU football fan appreciation day and had all the players sign it. We got a cart and my nephew took it to all the areas where the players were signing. They had the defensive guys together, they had the quarterbacks, the running backs – they were all over the stadium. And I've never seen a group of guys have so much fun signing something. My daughters would walk up to the players and ask, "Would you like to sign a toilet?" The players were laughing. At one time, they were all around the toilet, waiting to grab the pen so they could sign it. When we waited in

> **" Would you like to sign a toilet? "**

line for Coach Pinkel, we went up to him and he looked at the toilet and said, "I've never put my name on a toilet." He was laughing. I know Coach Pinkel has a charity and I want to get in touch with someone to donate a toilet to his charity. I'm really anxious to find out what the signed toilet went for – because all the players were saying how they wanted one and were asking where they could get one.

We did one special thing to the toilet that was auctioned off for the Children's Miracle Network – and I can't do it for any of the toilets I sell to the public. But at the bottom of the stool, there's a particular red and white bird decal that all the players were going crazy about. You can guess why? I put a coating over it so it would be there for the life of the toilet.

ROBERT RIPPY

Senior vice president, Robert W. Baird & Co., University of Missouri Class of 1974

A friend of mine went to a scrap dealer who had the two scoreboards from the old stadium on the University of Missouri campus. They were about nine feet by three feet and one said MISSOURI and the other said TIGERS. Well, my friend paid a good sum of money for the scoreboards, hoping they would fit in his house somewhere. But he had a winding stairway that led down to his basement and they just wouldn't fit. So he called me and asked if I would be

Robert Rippy had his home designed to display segments of the old Mizzou stadium scoreboard. Here he poses with the "Mizzou" half of the scoreboard.
Photo courtesy of Scott Thomas

interested in them. I told him I would, but I knew they wouldn't fit anywhere in my house, either. I had a friend who stored them in a warehouse for me.

Well, when my wife and I decided to build a new house, guess what I made sure would happen? That those scoreboards would fit downstairs. In the design, the blueprints called for two big windows downstairs, but we turned those windows into the two scoreboards from the old stadium. The windows were supposed to be on the east wall, and I told the architect that I had plans for that east wall. I think he thought I was crazy. He told me, "I've never put any scoreboards in a home before." And I knew he meant it because he had to come up with a plan to hang them. He made a frame and a box and we hung 27 square feet worth of scoreboards downstairs in the family room. I have some sports memorabilia downstairs, but it's the scoreboards that add the "Wow!" effect. They're a little bit weathered, but I didn't want to change anything about them. They are just like they were when they appeared at the old stadium. My wife can't stand to look at them, but she has all the upstairs to look at. I remember the first time I saw those old scoreboards, back in 1969. What a year – the Chiefs won the Super Bowl, Missouri was the Big 8 champion, and I saw the scoreboards – that would wind up in my family room – for the first time.

> **"I've never put any scoreboards in a home before."**

KRYSTEN CHAMBROT

This article is reprinted with the permission of The Missourian.

For many founding members, being an Antler is a lifelong sport.

Years after graduating from MU, a founding member of the Antlers, John "The Bicycle Repairman" Miller, went down to the Mizzou basketball court to yell at an official after MU lost a game at the buzzer.

Miller became so excited that the stitches from his recent wisdom teeth surgery broke. He continued to yell at the official even as drops of blood fell from his mouth.

"There was a lot of yelling going on," he said. "I don't think I ever got the attention of the official, but some people along press row were kind of terrified."

His fiancée watched from the stands.

"She married me nonetheless," he said.

Since their creation in 1976, the Antlers, a rowdy, organized fan group, have been scrutinized for their antics. In 1985, the group mocked then-Oklahoma coach Billy Tubbs. Tubbs had been struck by a hit-and-run driver. The group made a cardboard car that it paraded around Hearnes Center and pretended to hit a fellow Antler dressed as a jogger.

Another time, the Antlers waved a hog's head on a pole in front of then-Arkansas coach Nolan Richardson and his team. Over time, reports of the story have varied from the Antlers spilling pig's blood on Richardson's suit to brandishing several hogs' heads.

The group also came under fire for comments member Seth Rollins made about former Oklahoma coach Kelvin Sampson's daughter. At a game against Oklahoma, Rollins made mocking mention of Sampson's daughter being used as a recruiting tool.

Some folks considered the remark "over the line."

But Miller and five other one-time Antlers think their antics were all in good fun.

Miller, along with Jeff "Ramone the K" Gordon; Rob "The Hammer" Banning; "Jungle" George Stoecklin; Roger Geary; and John "Phlogdo of the Ozone" Shouse, were growing weary of the polite atmosphere at basketball games during the 1970s.

> There were two Jayhawk fans going to Six Flags over Texas. They were really excited because they had never been there before. They were driving along when they saw a sign that said, "Six Flags Left." So they turned around and went home.

"At most games during the week, there were seven to eight thousand people there, and you could hear a pin drop," Gordon said. "Three guys could distract a team because no one was doing anything."

They set out to make that happen by providing their support in unconventional ways.

The Antlers drew from sketch comedies of the 1970s. "Monty Python and The Holy Grail" influenced their performance, while "Saturday Night Live" gave them their name. In an episode of "Saturday Night Live," Lily Tomlin danced with her hands at the side of her head, fingers outstretched like she had antlers. As Gordon and Banning watched it, an idea was born. At one of their first games as an official group, the Antlers orchestrated their dance during the "Missouri Waltz."

While most attendees swayed their arms side-to-side above their heads, the Antlers wobbled, hands at their heads. Others took note and laughed. Soon the group became known as the Antlers.

The audience's reaction was mixed.

"There's always been the same reaction – some people were amused, some don't know what to make of us," Miller said.

Stoecklin said that while the Antlers were not the first overzealous fan group in the country, they were the first in the Midwest.

"Players that came from opposing teams did pay attention to us," he said. "I think we did affect games, however slightly."

Banning agreed.

"We like to think that we got a couple of points in the Tigers' favor," he said.

For years, the group taunted players and prided itself on securing the best seats in the Hearnes Center: section A-16. At one point, the Antlers pitched their tents in front of the Hearnes Center for eight days in November to secure tickets. Janet Shouse, wife of Antler John Shouse, said that the Antlers would camp out for long periods of time, even when attendance to basketball games waned.

"Nobody else showed up," she said. "They camped out for no reason other than to show their enthusiasm to Mizzou basketball."

MU's Athletic Department gave the group two rows of A-16 after it signed a sportsmanship agreement, restricting the use of profanity, to secure the seats. In 1995, the athletic department, citing the group's consistent behavior problem, suspended the group for a year and put the seats in the student lottery. The next year, the Antlers moved back to A-16. Since then, they have continued to face problems with their seating arrangements.

Although the Antlers were sometimes known for their obnoxious behavior, all of the founding members graduated with high GPAs. They have since become successful engineers, attorneys, veterinarians, and journalists.

Gordon graduated from MU in 1979 and writes Gordo's Zone, an online sports column for the *St. Louis Post-Dispatch*. He said he fell into sports writing while at MU and thinks his Antler days helped his career in sports talk radio. He said he looks back on the Antlers as a fraternity he and his friends created.

"As time goes on, you have kids and you hear from each other once in awhile," Gordon said. "You get a job, get married, have kids, and do your best to behave at games."

He keeps in touch with a couple of the Antlers, especially Banning.

Banning, who got his nickname, "The Hammer," from his ability to scream loudly for a long time without becoming hoarse, runs a plastics consulting and design company in St. Louis.

Banning said he never left the Antlers. After graduating with a degree in mechanical engineering in 1979, he came back several times to sit with the group. Banning admires the group's longevity.

"They're still there 30 years later," Banning said. "I have kids the same age as the Antlers. That alone makes me feel a little bit older."

Miller and Geary are attorneys in Kansas City. They still attend MU men's basketball games but do not participate in the Antlers' activities, anymore.

"Jungle" George Stoecklin, who got his nickname for his love of animals, is a veterinarian in Las Vegas. He stayed with the Antlers until he graduated in 1983 and opened his own practice where he treats small and exotic animals. Stoecklin's brother became an Antler over a decade later.

Shouse, an Antler from 1976 to 1982, is an engineering manager for an industrial automation company in Nashville, Tennessee. He met his wife while in line for MU basketball tickets. She was a season ticket holder in college and sat a section away from the Antlers.

Janet Shouse attributes their 21-year marriage to John's involvement in the Antlers.

"If he had been a typical spectator, I would've never seen him," she said. Janet Shouse said her husband was shy outside of his Antler persona.

"He was very different from what I'd see in the basketball arena, and then what I saw when we went out," she said.

John Shouse said he stays in contact with his fellow Antlers, including Cathy Boyd, the first female Antler.

Since leaving college, many of the original members still have their Antler values, even if they can't fit into their black and gold T-shirts.

Some of the former Antlers have kept up with each season's Antlers over the years. Gordon said the current Antlers are under more pressure than the Antlers of his era.

"Norm Stewart loved us, so we could get away with murder," he said. "We had a free run of the place, and it was a different time, before political correctness."

MU's Faculty Council recently dropped a proposal to regulate fan behavior after the Antlers' actions at a game in 2005 against Indiana University. The council dropped the proposal after it found out Tad Dunn, director of game operations, had sent the group an e-mail about its behavior.

Faculty Council member Rex Campbell drew up the proposal last month.

"Some members of the Antlers make some very awkward comments about persons from other communities,"

Campbell said. "I don't mind razzing, but when you personalize it, it's uncalled for."

Chad Moller, director of media relations for the athletic department, did not specifically single out the Antlers but did discuss fan behavior in general.

"Whenever something happens that crosses the line, we do our best to deal with that," he said.

Stewart said he liked the Antlers because they made basketball games more fun. He keeps in touch with Miller and Geary.

"All of those guys showed a lot of imagination, a lot of creativity, and they were also controllable," he said. "Sometimes they lost it, but they would still come back to center."

Geary described the Antlers' harassing as a mingling of art and science.

"It's a combination of journalistic research techniques combined with psychology and theater when it's done well," he said.

The Antlers take teasing seriously. Since its early days, the group's code has not allowed drinking on game days.

"You have to be on for three-and-a-half hours," Gordon said. "You can't be sharp if you're drunk."

Geary said some might not believe the Antlers were serious about their jest and grew up to be serious adults.

"Perhaps surprising to some, we have generally blended into the normal population fairly effectively," he said.

Despite this, some of the founding Antlers do not repress their avid fandom.

"I find myself hollering at the TV all the time," Shouse said.

Gordon does, too. He said he sometimes has flashbacks to his Antler days at his children's sporting events. His wife has to keep him in line from time to time, he said.

"Sometimes she has to slap me and tell me to shut up," he said.

His wife agrees. She knew many of the Antlers while attending graduate school at MU, when they looked out for her. Years later, she notes how the Antler-like behavior never left her husband.

"The Antlers are very much alive," she said.

ANTLER HIGHLIGHTS:

* Prior to a Missouri-Kansas basketball game in 2003, members of the Antlers called former KU coach Roy Williams at his home at 2:27 a.m., 2:45 a.m., and 3:05 a.m. Williams told the *Lawrence Journal World*, "I said, 'Fellas, it's not going to get started tonight,' and I just hung up. They called a second time and I hung up. The third time I heard loud music in the background. It sounded like it was a pretty good establishment, and they were having a good time. I don't sleep, anyway. They are not disturbing me; they might as well call at noon."

* Before that same game, members of the Antlers greeted the KU players at their hotel in Columbia, holding up signs that read: "Plane Crash." The sign was in reference to former KU player Nick Collison's Senior Day speech, when he talked about his grandfather – a World War II veteran whose plane crashed during D-Day. (He survived.)

* In 2005, Baylor coach Scott Drew invited an Antler into his team's locker room before a game against the Tigers to dare him to repeat what he and his fellow Antlers had said to the team the night before while they were eating at a restaurant. "Basically, the coach told me that what he wanted me to do was say how bad they suck and how we're going to kick their ass," Michael Booth, the one chosen for the pre-game talk, told the *Columbia Daily Tribune.* Missouri won the game.

* The Antlers enjoyed taking on visiting columnists, if they happened to be the negative subjects of a column. While Colorado's Glean Eddy was attempting a free throw at a home game in 2005, the Antlers chanted the name of columnist Tony Messenger, letting him know what they thought of his writing skills.

* Before the 1994 Braggin' Rights game against Illinois, the Antlers sent Illinois guard Kiwane Garris two bricks in the mail. These were references to his two missed free throws with no time left at the end of regulation in the epic 1993 battle that Missouri won in three overtimes.

* The Antlers posed as fans of Iowa State center Dean Uthoff and called his dorm room to say they wanted to send him a pizza. They told him it would be in the lobby in a half hour. It's reported that Uthoff waited more than an hour for the pizza before he realized that he had been scammed. At the game, when Iowa State visited Missouri, the Antlers waved empty pizza boxes at Uthoff.

* An Antler dressed like Bob Knight when Missouri played host to the coach's Texas Tech team in 2007. The Knight impersonator walked through the Antlers and began punching them, parodying Knight's reputation.

* The Antlers caught some heat for holding up a poster of Larry Brown, the legendary Kansas coach, next to a poster of Libyan dictator Moammar Khadafy. Another poster read: "Which one's the terrorist?"

* Perhaps the most infamous Antler sign was caught by a cameraman on a nationally televised Missouri-Arkansas game. It simply read:

> **Corey**
> **Beck has**
> **Syphilis**

* Security guards took away an Antler's sign on December 9, 2002, during Missouri's win over Wisconsin-Green Bay. The sign featured the names of two Phoenix players, Calix N'Daiye and Derek Schiedt. It read: **Eat Schiedt N'Daiye**. Think about it for a moment …

RICH MONTGOMERY

University of Missouri, Class of 1967

I am celebrating my 40th anniversary of being a member of the Missouri football "chain gang" (the game officials who manage the 10-yard measurements, downs, and line of scrimmage).

I used to carry the pistol for the referee to signal the end of a quarter – that was a long time ago. When people hear that I have worked the chain gang for 40 years, they want to know about the five-down Colorado game – back in 1990. It's one I'll never forget and neither will any MU or Colorado fan. To this day, I don't know how it happened, and neither do a lot of folks.

On first and goal, their quarterback, Charles Johnson, spiked the ball to stop the clock. On second down, Eric Bienemy carried the ball and was stopped short of the end zone. Colorado called timeout. Their back carried the ball again, and was stopped short, and for some reason, everybody still had second down – including me. Johnson then spiked the ball – on fourth down – but we all had third down. The drive was over, but, like everyone knows, they got one more chance.

On fifth down, Johnson carried the ball and reaches across the goal line. He was stopped short. To this day, I know he was stopped short, but he rolled over and reached into the end zone and it was called a touchdown and Colorado won the game. The *St. Louis Post-Dispatch* ran a great picture showing he was short. Some poor guy up in the stands had a heart attack, and emergency people were working on him – all the MU kids were down on the sidelines ready to storm the field, thinking they were going to beat Colorado. It was just unbelievable.

Somehow, we ran the second down twice and they used the five plays to (eventually) win a National Championship. Don Dimry, the head linesman, was so upset over the whole thing he had a nervous breakdown. That one drive really changed some destiny that year as it would have been a huge win for Missouri and who knows, Colorado probably wouldn't have won the National Championship.

I was lucky that I never caught a lot of heck for it, even though I was on the down marker. But it sure affected some of the officials. My son, Jeff, went to Missouri and coached the Tigers and he went to a clothing store in Columbia and they had a down marker with a No. 5 on it. He wanted to get that for me, so he asked if they would sell it to him. They didn't sell it to him – they gave it to him. I still have it. That's something that wouldn't happen once out of 9 million, 900 and 99 plays – but it happened that day and people still talk about it. Years later, my wife and I were on a cruise and we were taking a ferry boat to a store and a guy was talking and said he was from Colorado. Another guy asked him about that Colorado game with five downs – and here I was, sitting a few feet away from them, just listening to the conversation.

My Missouri experiences are priceless and I treasure every one of them, with the exception of that one.

SCOTT LUCAS

University of Missouri, Class of 1978

Most people remember where they were when President Kennedy was shot or when the Twin Towers fell. Sports fans will always remember the 1980 Olympic hockey team and the Miracle on Ice. For Mizzou fans, there are many wins that stick out, but for me the loss I will always remember is the loss to Nebraska on the deflected pass. I was at home watching the game on television. As the game progressed, I gained more confidence that this would be a Tiger victory over the Cornhuskers. Late in the game we were ahead and seemed to be in control. It would only take one more defensive stop for us to pull off the upset.

Back in those days, our football team had pulled off some great upsets. We beat a top-ranked Southern Cal team, as well as a top-ranked Notre Dame team. We had also beaten

Alabama and Ohio State on the road. I remember those road wins especially. Back then when the football team had a big win on the road, all the students on campus would head to the "columns." It would be a mass of people celebrating the win.

So as the (Nebraska) game wound down, I started to believe that we had this one in the bag. Unfortunately, that was short lived. Nebraska was running out of time and was forced to pass. Our defense had played a great game, but needed to come through one more time. It took a miracle play on a broken pass for them to pull off the miracle. In the closing seconds, our defense toughened and deflected a pass that was a sure reception. However, an alert Nebraska running back picked the ball out of mid-air and scored the touchdown. It was Nebraska's version of the Pittsburgh Steelers' "Immaculate Reception."

As the play occurred, I was down on my hands and knees pounding the floor in anguish. I was totally oblivious to the fact that my 6-year-old son was still in the room. As I am yelling in frustration and hitting the floor, my son gets up and runs out of the room. He ran straight upstairs to my wife. He tells her between sniffles that "Daddy is scaring me." My wife came downstairs and, let's just say, gave me a dirty look.

We had been invited to a party later that night. The ride to the party was not very warm as you could have cut the tension in the car between my wife and I. At the party, the wives started discussing how their husbands had acted during the football game that afternoon. As it turns out, I actually handled myself much better than a number of my friends. That really helped me on the ride home. My wife forgave me and I promised never to pound the ground again during a Mizzou football game. Not sure if I have been able to keep that promise, but at least it never happened in front of my son again.

Now things have come full circle. My son is a freshman at Mizzou. He carries on a long family tradition. Both my brothers and sister went to Mizzou, as did all of their kids. All told, 14 people from my family have gone to Mizzou. My Tiger roots run deep and I can't be held responsible for how I act during a tough game. It's in my blood.

KURT MIRTSCHING

University of Missouri, Class of 1981, "Director of Everything" and CEO of iconic eatery in Columbia, Shakespeare's Pizza

I just call myself the director of everything at Shakespeare's. It just kind of fits, because I do everything and I love it. This place has been around since 1973 and is as special to me now as it was when I was dating my wife. She went to school in St. Louis and I asked her if she wanted to go get some pizza. We drove from St. Louis to Columbia, and she asked, "Are you crazy?" I am. But she still married me. What was really crazy was back then, Shakespeare's didn't even have a dining room. They just had carry out, so we got our pizza and ate it on the way back to St. Louis. A true story – honest to God.

People always associate us with MU sports, which is great. But did you know that (world renowned philharmonic conductor) Zubin Mehta was appearing at Jesse Hall and asked for some pizza and he got Shakespeare's? The same thing happened with Mel Blanc, the voice of Bugs Bunny and all those great old cartoon characters. He was giving a lecture at Jesse Hall and he asked for some great pizza and they brought him Shakespeare's.

Carl Edwards is a regular whenever he's in town. Long before he became a big NASCAR driver, he came into Shakespeare's and he was wearing jeans and a ratty T-shirt. He and a buddy rode their bikes from Carl's house and he got here and was asking about our pedi-cabs – they're kind of like a rickshaw and we pay kids to drive them around town for advertisement. So we ask him if he's interested in a part-time job, driving one of our pedi-cabs around town. You could see he was trying to keep from laughing, and he said that it sounded like a cool job and that he'd consider it. Well, we found out later we were talking to Carl Edwards and we were so embarrassed. The next time he came in, we apologized and he said that no apology was necessary. "That was as funny as hell," Edwards said.

> "We ran a special saying that you'd get so much money off a pizza for an A, B, or C on a final exam, but that you would get it free if you flunked. We got a letter from an administrator at Stephens College saying that we were making a mockery out of higher education."

Bill Cosby had our pizza before a performance and we asked him to wear a Shakespeare's T-shirt and he did. And he said he loved our pizza. I guess a comedian would like our pizza since we don't really take ourselves too seriously. We've been on (Jay) Leno a couple of times and (David)

Mizzou's iconic pizza place – Shakespeare's.
Photo courtesy of Rich Zvosec

Letterman with our ads. We had one that said we make our own window cleaner and Letterman said, "I used to go to Pizza Hut until I found out they use that store-bought stuff." Leno talked about, "Shakespeare's Pizza? Chop sticks? At a pizza place?" We got a lot of attention for that one. And then we ran a special saying that you'd get so much money off a pizza for an A, B, or C on a final exam, but that you would get it free if you flunked. We got a letter from an administrator at Stephens College saying that we were making a mockery out of higher education. Excuse me? Have you ever heard of a JOKE! We like to have fun and we're proud of our pizza.

GABRIELA LESSA

The Missourian

Shakespeare's Pizza has a relaxed atmosphere, with its clever signs (you don't need to clean your table because "this is not the dorm"), towel napkins, and friendly staff.

And, of course, classic pizza.

At least 15,000 students hit the place every year to eat, and many come back after they graduate. This loyalty is documented by the wall of pictures showing customers in Shakespeare's Pizza shirts all over the world.

You can even have pizza mailed to you anywhere in America. A few customers have paid up to $80 to have Shakespeare's ship a pizza to their kitchens.

Tony and Bill Wrisinger, and their mother, Jan, have a lifetime worth of memories of the late Frank Wrisinger

Smiles, nods of approval, and good-natured slaps on the back are not sights one often associates with the funeral of a good friend.

But this wasn't your typical memorial visitation.

As Frank Wrisinger's friends and family members filed past his casket, they found out – if they didn't already know – that the University of Missouri held a special place in their late friend's heart for more than 73 years.

"Dad wanted to wear his MU gear – right down to his Tiger slippers – in his final resting place, so we made sure he had on his MU shirt and had all the things he would watch the game with the past few years," said his son, Tony.

Wrisinger, left, and his son, Bill, enjoy a special father-son moment at the 1997 Holiday Bowl.
Photo courtesy of Tony Wrisinger

"It was interesting to watch the reactions of the folks who walked past Dad's casket when they saw him in his MU shirt. They all got a good smile out of it. It was a sad occasion, but it was also a happy occasion, because we knew that Dad would be wearing the same gear when he was in heaven cheering for the Tigers."

Tony's brother, Bill, said, "We had a Tiger tail hanging out of the casket and one of Dad's friends, a KU fan, wore his KU shirt to the funeral. I don't think Dad would have minded because he knew what it was like to be a fan, a real fan."

Whenever MU was playing a big game, Frank went through a routine.

"Frank would fly his MU flag," said his wife, Jan. "And I'm going to keep that tradition alive. I think Frank would have liked that and I know my boys like it – so do the grandkids."

Jan Wrisinger's home is replete with MU gear that dates back to the days when Frank was a young Tiger fan.

"This Tiger footstool has to be 40 or 50 years old," Jan said. "Frank used this footstool for every game he watched. Just look at it – you can see how old it is. Now, the grandkids sit on it and enjoy the games."

There are Tiger photos, autographs, pillows, rugs, tissue dispensers, and memorabilia that still hold a special place in the heart of the Wrisingers.

"You know," Tony said, "I can look at all the Tiger memorabilia and see my Dad sitting in his favorite chair, with his feet up on that footstool, watching the game and cheering for his Tigers.

"That's a memory we will have for the rest of our lives."

Chase Knocks 'em Dead

The upper level of the shopping mall looked more like the site of a Mizzou pep rally.

The walkway was filled with thousands of black and gold, card-carrying University of Missouri football fans – well, make that card-carrying Chase Daniel fans.

"We want Chase! We want Chase!" chanted 9-year-old Robbie Magruder, his younger brother, Austin, and their cousin, Will, as they waited for Daniel, the most prolific quarterback in University of Missouri history.

Sisters Sara Magruder and Beth Fox and their three boys were the first in line to meet Daniel, who has become the face of Mizzou football in recent years.

"We got here early," Beth Fox said. "Can you imagine us trying to corral these three guys in the middle of a line? We needed some wide open spaces, so we figured we'd better be first."

Right behind the Magruders and Foxes was 13-year-old Cole Sales, who brought his own camera to document the event.

"My uncle told me about this and I just had to come meet Chase Daniel," said Sales. "He's the best quarterback I ever saw and I wanted to meet him."

With Robbie, Austin, and Will chanting, "M-I-Z..." and the "Z-O-U!" response coming from the other side of the shopping center, Daniel made an appearance. He was a few minutes late - fashionably late, by celebrity standards – but when he sat behind a desk to sign a variety of fan items, the place burst into applause.

Mark Patek, Tiger Town owner and former Missouri football and baseball player, said he knew Daniel would attract a large crowd.

"We've had Jeremy Maclin and Chase Coffman (together) and Tony Temple," Patek said, "and the fans have really turned out. Chase is the face of MU football, so I'm not at all surprised at how many people showed up."

Daniel signed helmets, footballs, photos, posters, and even an infant MU one-piece outfit that a dad immediately placed on his infant daughter.

Daniel signed every autograph for every person in line, posed for hundreds of photos, hugged more babies than a politician, and seemed to be having the time of his life.

"Chase really appreciates his fans," said Daniel's girlfriend, Blaire Vandiver. "I like coming to events like this because Chase is so personable. He makes sure that everyone who comes through to see him gets some personal attention."

SARA MAGRUDER

University of Missouri Class of 1996

What do I love about the University of Missouri? It would be easier and quicker to say what I didn't love when I went to school in Columbia because I loved everything about my Mizzou experience.

I'm a sports nut, so all the sporting events were great. The football team wasn't as successful as it is now, but it was still so much fun to go to games. But if I had to pick one event, one thing that stands out in my mind, it would be

Homecoming. The whole town, the entire Greek community, all the visitors, it was just something you can't really describe unless you see it in person. All the frat houses would put on displays and have little mini-plays on the house decks; they had skits, it was colorful, and the streets were just crawling with people.

The parade on Homecoming day was always so colorful and I remember how people would line up along the parade route hours before so they could sit in their lawn chairs and watch it all unfold. It didn't matter if you were young or old, a Missouri alum or student or parent or visitor, it was a spectacle.

Every little girl would be wearing an MU cheerleader outfit and every little boy would be wearing a Tiger football jersey with his favorite player's number. And on that day, it didn't matter what the team's record was because Homecoming was so special, such a great event, you just felt like you were lucky to be a Tiger.

And for a farm girl going to Mizzou, it was something that shocked and amazed me. I'd never seen anything like it. I still go back as often as I can, and I loved to go watch Chase Daniel and the Mizzou football team the past three years. Now, my kids are big MU fans and even bigger Chase Daniel fans. Why else do you think I'd stand in line over four hours so they could meet him and get his autograph? We're fanatics.

BETH FOX

University of Missouri Class of 1990

When I went to Missouri back in 1990, I wanted to experience it all. I still remember getting the freshman orientation packet that had all the things that were really important – like my pass to all the sporting events. I grew up on a farm in Odessa, Missouri, and I knew that I was going to have to work hard to survive. But I had a strong work ethic because I knew when I was growing up, if the chores didn't get done, there would be some serious consequences.

I really got involved in dorm life and followed all the sports teams. I worked the front desk and got a job in the Instructional Material Lab, which was part of my major. When you work anywhere in the university, it's like you have 20 mothers looking after you and I always appreciated their concern and how they took care of me. I think I was a junior when I really got involved in the sports programs, and now, with my two boys (and one daughter) we are really into MU sports. It's kind of ironic that my first teaching job was in Hallsville, Missouri, and we brought some students to the MU football games to sell concessions as a fund raiser. It's amazing how much Missouri and the sports teams at Missouri have been, and always will be, a part of my life and my family's life. I'm so lucky to be a Tiger.

TRAVIS SCOTT

University of Missouri, Class of 2007

I'm sure people were wondering why my family, with so many youngsters among the group, would wait for hours to meet Chase Daniel at his appearance at Tiger Town. The five of us, myself, my wife, Kristin Scott, our oldest son, Blake Vance, who is 6, our middle son, Dalton Vance, who is 4, and our youngest at two months, Chase Scott, waited in line that day. I was excited to see how anxious the boys were to meet their favorite football player and the namesake of their baby brother. We brought a onsie for Chase to sign. We only waited in line for about an hour and a half; we expected longer. It was awesome to see everyone there, all with their own stories about why they loved Chase Daniel and Mizzou football. There were so many people with so many different things awaiting his signature. The time seemed to fly by, though, with so many things to keep us entertained in line with our children. The older two children were asking questions about Chase such as, "Does Chase like football?" "Does Chase know you named our baby his name?" And more importantly, "Why did you name Chase his name, do you know him?" Then we had to explain the reason for his name.

When Kristin and I met, we were both going to school at MU and working on campus at the same place. After I graduated in May of 2007 we moved back to the Kansas City area. When we found out we were having a boy for our first child together, we wanted to give Chase a name that had a good deal of meaning in our lives. We already had a boy that starts with 'B' and one with 'D', so we wanted one that was

Mizzou's Chase Daniel with a namesake, little Chase Daniel Scott.
Photo courtesy of Travis Scott

near their names, so we decided to have a name that started with a 'C'. When Kristin suggested Chase, I was thrilled. In that same conversation I told my wife "I will agree to Chase only if his middle name can be Daniel." At first, we were only half serious; it didn't sound right to name him after someone we haven't actually met, but the more we talked about how great it sounded, and of course all the wonderful memories we share from MU, it only made more sense to keep it and name him Chase Daniel Scott. Once we decided that was his name, there was no changing our minds.

Having (the "big") Chase take a picture with our Chase will be a story we can share for years, not to mention what a huge inspiration he has been for my other two children.

When you meet someone you admire, and he turns out to be even classier and nicer than you expected, it is special. Chase is definitely my favorite player at Missouri. I was lucky enough to go to school at the time when the Missouri football program reached a high point in its history. I believe that Chase played a part in that. But I'm not just a big fan of Chase; I'm a big fan of Missouri football in general.

MATT GERSTNER

University of Missouri student

One thing I've realized with Missouri Tiger fans is how persistent they really are. If they want something, they're determined to get it. I'm honored to share this trait with my fellow black-and-gold bleeders.

I've been a Mizzou fan my whole life. My first Missouri game was after a football game with my little league team that just happened to be named the Tigers. My dad, who is a diehard Iowa fan but who has learned to welcome the Tigers into his cold heart (that's a joke), took me to the Bowling Green game in 1997, in which the Tigers shut out the Falcons, 37-0. From that moment on, I loved Mizzou.

Almost every year after that we went to at least one game, mostly non-conference games against teams like UAB, and a couple against Bowling Green, although the Tigers lost one of those games in pretty sad fashion.

The Tigers were pretty sad themselves for a while. But the fans kept coming. Football and basketball. They kept lining up at the doors. Any time there's a slump, the fans still stay behind the team.

That's persistence that a lot of colleges don't see. And I think I joined the ranks of the diehards with the most recent case of Mizzou rejoicing in a Kansas defeat. I won't lie, it was probably the most exciting basketball game I will ever be witness to in my life.

For the 2008-09 season, I worked for Metro Sports (TV) as, well, a lackey, holding cords, wrapping cords, lugging cases, that kind of thing. Not that I'm complaining. I did get $50 and courtside seats for the Mizzou non-conference basketball games. They would hand out these pink slips that served as our press passes.

For students, getting Kansas tickets was difficult. For this Border War, which featured probably the most hyped Missouri team, my girlfriend, Tammy Mullins, really wanted to go, as did my roommate, Kofi Oyirifi. Kofi found a ticket from a friend who had a test that night, because his teacher lived under a rock or something, so he was set.

I really wanted Tammy to go, but I knew there was no way in hell she'd let me give up my ticket just so she could go. So I figured I could use my press pass to get in like I did for all the other games and I'd be set.

My friends, I think they totaled about 12, went in two other cars, and I took Kofi and Tammy in my car, as my press pass was in there.

Of course, I get to my car, and the pink slip isn't in there. Tammy and I are freaking. Again, I offered to give up my ticket to make up for my lapse in intelligence, which she promptly refused.

So I have this hair-brained idea to go in the back of the arena, with my hoodie zipped up, and hope nobody will ask questions.

So we parked in front of the football training facility, walked across the Tiger Walk bridge, and up the hill that runs in front of the arena. I wound around the back, to see just about every broadcast truck in the Midwest parked behind the arena, and I think I hyperventilated.

I went in through the back door, trying not to look conspicuous, although just the fact that I was thinking about it probably made me look conspicuous. I had to run to the bathroom and actually had to wait, which I figured would just ruin my chances. Mark DeArmond, Missouri writer for *The Kansas City Star* and one of my personal favorites, comes out of the bathroom, and I have to fight the urge to introduce myself, in fear that my cover would be blown.

I come out to the court as both teams are wrapping up their shootarounds. To say the place was a madhouse would be an understatement. Gold. Huge amounts of gold were all you could see in the stands. At this point I'm thinking, "No way in hell is this going to work out. It's just too perfect."

And then, the hardest part came next.

I have to walk up the center aisle through the Antlers, the courtside cameras, and just about anybody who could get me thrown out with a simple point to the ushers. Needless to say, my heart was in my ribs, throat, and stomach, simultaneously.

And yet for some reason, my luck came through again in the clutch. Nobody asked a question. Miraculously, I make it up to the concourse, meet up with the rest of the party, and just wait for the game to start.

The first half was, as the records will show, terrible. I think we were down 16 or 17, if not worse, at halftime. We all wondered if we even should have shown up for the game.

The second half was, as the records will show, epic.

Mizzou dominated the floor, Zaire Taylor hit the game winner with 0.8 seconds left, every guy picks up their girl and kisses them, and everybody rushes the court, including us. It was mayhem.

Never in my life have I experienced so much excitement, tension, disappointment, hope, fear, elation, and overall bliss at any other sporting event.

There's just something about the Border War that brings out every side of people. It's unlike anything you'll ever witness.

DR. JIM WHITAKER

University of Missouri defensive back from 1963-66 and renowned orthopedic surgeon who has worked with the Kansas City Chiefs, Kansas City Wizards, and old Kansas City Kings

I grew up going to Catholic schools and was probably more groomed to go to a place like Notre Dame. In fact, I visited there twice. But my father thought it would be a good idea to get around girls and go to a secular school. And I wanted to go to a place that had good football. That is a big reason I chose Missouri. As I look back, I can see in so many ways that the impact of the relationships with my teammates and coaches has affected my life in a positive manner.

Playing for Coach (Dan) Devine was very intimidating. My sophomore year, I get a chance to play because Johnny Roland got tired. Back then you played both ways, and he was the starting running back and defensive back. I was the relief man for Roland. I remember playing against California back when they had Craig Morton, who went on to play in the NFL. Devine thought if we could control the ball on the ground with Roland, then we could win. Unfortunately, that meant I was thrown into the fire for the first time. It felt like he had a thousand yards that day.

More memorable is the fact that it was my first flight. It was the first time many of my teammates had been on a plane, as well. One of my best friends on the team, Lloyd Carr, had never been on a plane, either. (Yes, that is the Lloyd Carr of Michigan fame. He played two years at Missouri before transferring with Assistant Coach Rollie

Dodge when Dodge got his first head coaching job at Northern Michigan.) There were a lot of scared football players on the plane that day. Overall, it was a great experience.

Off the field, I had an opportunity to play against the St. Louis Cardinals. I got a call one Sunday morning from Assistant Coach Clay Cooper who told me to get down to the fieldhouse as we were heading to St. Louis to play the Cardinals in a charity basketball game. I found myself playing that morning against guys like Jerry Stovall and Larry Wilson in a basketball game. That afternoon we went to the stadium and watched them play in an NFL game. Don't think that would happen today. I don't remember who won, but I do remember that they were a little bit better athletes.

During my time at MU, the people who had the most impact on me were not my professors, but the coaches. Clay Cooper was the defensive backs coach and was a hero to me. He was a great player at MU and a very learned man. He set the bar high for us both on and off the field. I developed a father-son type relationship with him and never wanted to let him down. This was a culture that Devine helped foster, as well.

Coach Devine was a little bit aloof when you played for him, but after graduation you knew you could always count on him. I will never forget when I was doing my residency in Indiana and he called me in the middle of surgery. He wanted me to come up to a game and help him recruit. He even asked me to help recruit my younger brother, Bill. Coach made sure that I was in South Bend when he came to visit. What he didn't know is, that at the end of the visit, it didn't matter what I said. Bill thought that the girls at Mizzou were much prettier and that sealed the deal. Another trademark of Coach Devine was that he would always hire his former players to be his assistants.

Later, I was very proud of the fact that I was one of the people who helped bring Coach Devine back to be the athletic director at Mizzou. When he came back, you could really see how popular he was with the Tiger supporters.

Another memorable experience I had after graduation was being invited back to the alumni game. The alumni game was a tradition back then and lasted until the early 1970s. I think it finally ended after someone had a heart attack or got hurt. For a number of years after I graduated, they would call me and ask me to come back. I had always declined due to other obligations. Finally, after putting them off with time conflicts, I was "guilted" into playing one year. Now let me give you the whole picture. Back in those days, former players like myself would come back for the weekend and play the actual varsity team. On Friday, we would arrive and be fitted with helmets and pads. Then we would go out and have a practice. After practice, we headed over to the local bar to get reacquainted with each other. Then someone would bring out the old 16mm game films of our glory days. We sat there and relived some great moments while tossing back a few beers. The conversation would drift from those games to how we were going to beat the varsity team the next day. I knew that was crazy talk because we had all seen the players after our practice. They were big and in shape and we were, let's just say, not in as good of shape. Quite frankly, I just wanted to get through the game without getting hurt.

I can still see Coach Faurot coming into the locker room at halftime as we were all shooting the breeze. He stepped up to the chalkboard and started diagramming plays and telling us how if we executed better on offense and got better coverage in the secondary that we could win the game. Coach Faurot was treating this as the Super Bowl. I loved his passion and competitive spirit, but it didn't have enough of an impact on a group of guys who were no longer living and dying on each play.

Life came full circle for me as all three of my daughters went to Mizzou. And now that I have a little more time, I have even volunteered to be the defensive coordinator for the St. Ann's fourth grade football team. I guess my former Mizzou coaches are still having an impact on me.

CHAPTER 4

We Broadcast the Game

Gary Link … Mike Kelly … John Kadlec …
when broadcasting Tiger games, their voices are
music to our ears.

GARY LINK

University of Missouri Class of 1974, former player and broadcaster

I was fortunate enough to play the last game in Brewer Hall and play in the first game in Hearnes Arena. Then I had a chance to broadcast the last game at Hearnes and the first game at Mizzou Arena. For a Missouri kid, that is really special. My dream growing up was to play at Missouri. Brewer Fieldhouse was a unique experience. Our locker room was OK, but the visiting team dressed in a weight room that had leaky pipes on the ceiling. After leaving the locker room, you had to walk across the dirt track and then before you came up the stairs to the floor, the visiting players would wipe their shoes off. At the end of the floor you had two cyclone fences to keep the ball from rolling away. I remember as a freshman watching the managers sweep the floor and hammering down all the loose nails in the floor. There were games where the action would stop so that the manager could pound down any nails that popped up. All that being said, it was a great place to play. To me, that place was magic!

Every year we would play in the Big 8 Christmas tournament. It was a special time because of the camaraderie we developed playing and watching other teams play over the three days of the event. You stayed in the Muehlbach Hotel (in Kansas City) and went through an underground tunnel to Municipal Auditorium where the games were played. We won the tournament three years in a row. In fact, Al Eberhard and I are the only players in Mizzou history to go 9-0 in that tournament.

> **"I remember as a freshman watching the managers sweep the floor and hammering down all the loose nails in the floor."**

Playing for Coach (Norm) Stewart was always exciting and he really appreciated the fact that he built the program with Missouri kids. One tournament I remember most was when we went to Tennessee. Back then, no one had special introductions, but they did. They would turn the lights off and hit each player with a spotlight as they were introduced. Coach Stewart decided to have some fun, so he told all the starters to scatter around the court. As the announcer introduced the first player, the guy running the spotlight pointed it toward the bench, but John Brown came running in from the corner. The poor spotlight could never catch up to a player coming in from a different spot. We were laughing, but the fans started booing even louder. The best part was that we beat them and won the tournament. As Coach Stewart said after the game, "We will never be invited back because we stole their gold watches by winning the tourney." I don't think Mizzou has ever been back to their tourney.

All the games against Kansas were memorable. I remember my junior year when we went over and John Brown led us to the win. Being from Dixon, Missouri, it was special for him. As I said before, it was special to be from small towns and cities in Missouri and have an opportunity to play here.

One game that sticks out during my time as a broadcaster is a game at Kansas when Brian Grawer, Clarence Gilbert, and Keyon Dooling were playing. We had lost to Colorado the week before and had a week to prepare. I will never forget Coach Stewart walking to the back of the bus and telling the players, "When we win, we will show them the proper respect." As I heard this I thought, "When we win? I just hope we don't get beat by 50."

With the outcome of the game decided (the Tigers were up), Brian Grawer runs over to the guys on the bench and reminds them of what Coach Stewart told us. After the game ended, we shook hands and went to the locker room. It wasn't until we got on the bus that the emotions took over the team. It was so emotional I thought the bus was going to explode. As I told Coach Stewart, "I played for you and have broadcast your games for years, but I never thought we would have a chance." It was a special moment to watch Brian repeat what Coach had told them on the bus. Now that is a great example of Mizzou sports and class.

One of the best things about playing at Mizzou was the people. Back when I played, there was a core group of people called the Tail Twisters – about 10 or 12 people who were friends of Coach Stewart and moms and dads who would look after you. If you needed a meal or someone to talk with, they were there. They were always there to support you. They were kind of like a "security blanket" when you were away from home. Many of them became lifelong friends. I think they really appreciated the fact that Coach Stewart always tried to bring in primarily Missouri kids.

MIKE KELLY

Voice of the Missouri Tigers since 1989

My association with Missouri sports started in 1989 when I was offered the opportunity to do Tiger Talk with head football coach Bob Stuhl. I was working at KMOX in

St. Louis and my general manager asked me if I wanted to drive to Columbia to do the show. I told him I would love to do it. That began my association with Mizzou.

One of the most memorable football moments for me was the Colorado game in 1997. It was an emotional win that guaranteed the first winning season for the Tigers in 14 years. Watching Coach (Larry) Smith celebrate the win with the long-time fans, they all had tears in their eyes from the pure joy that the victory brought.

There have been so many great moments for me doing Mizzou basketball, but one season that sticks out is the 1993-94 season. It started out questionable as we went down and opened up Bud Walton Arena at Arkansas. One of their players banks in a three-pointer to open the game and we lose big. Jon Sundvold was doing the color (commentary) with me and was sending me notes about how bad this game was going to end up and he was right.

However, the genius of Norm Stewart prevailed with this team. A couple of weeks later we beat Illinois in a triple-overtime game. It was a game that we were down big, but battled back and prevailed. That team would go undefeated in the Big 8. As Coach Stewart said after the year, "The sum of the parts is better than any one individual." One game that sticks out is when Kelly Thames hit a last-second shot over Bryant "Big Country" Reeves and we beat Oklahoma State. It was an incredible shot and preserved the undefeated conference season.

One thing about traveling and broadcasting games with Coach Stewart, you knew it was always going to be exciting. He was a master about softening up the opposing fans. I remember when we played Arkansas one year and Coach Stewart comes out early and goes into the stands and starts giving out books, ties, and candy to the students. Then when we played at Nebraska he had his players wear red T-shirts during warm-ups saying congratulations to Coach (Tom) Osborne for winning the (football) National Championship. The student section was all primed to boo us, but when the players shed their warm-up jackets and displayed the T-shirts, the place erupted in applause. I can only wonder what the Nebraska coach thought at that moment.

Why do KU graduates hang their diplomas on their rearview mirrors?

So they can park in the handicapped spot.

One thing about Mizzou fans that may be different from a lot of fans is that they are very appreciative of players who work hard. They like the "blue collar mentality." In other words, they want their team to work as hard on the field as they do to pay for their tickets to games.

CHAPTER 5

It's a Family Affair

"It's a Family Affair" features stories about athletes and what Mizzou means to them, along with accounts of their family members and what it means to watch them.

Dave Fry

Dave did not attend the University of Missouri, but his three sons – Shaon, Ryan, and Brett, were standouts in their respective sports.

If you read a novel or watched a feel-good, after-school movie about a family like this, you'd think to yourself, "This is too good to be true."

The Fry family really is too good to be true, but sometimes, reality works out that way.

Over a two-week span in 1999, longtime baseball coach Dave Fry and his son, Shaon, were inducted into their sports' respective halls of fame.

Dave, who has won two state championships at Fort Osage, was inducted into the Missouri High School Baseball Coaches Association Hall of Fame in Springfield.

Shaon was inducted into the University of Missouri Hall of Fame, where he was a nationally ranked wrestler and academic All-America for the Tigers.

But it doesn't end there.

In addition to the two state championships Dave won in 1991 and 1997, he also led his teams to four conference titles, five district championships, and three sectional crowns.

His eldest son, Shaon, a three-time state wrestling champion in high school, was ranked second in the nation (167 pounds) at the University of Missouri his junior year and third his senior year.

Dave's middle son, Ryan, pitched Oak Grove to its first Class 3A state baseball championship in 1992. He then set several hitting records at the University of Missouri and was drafted by the Kansas City Royals and played for a year in their organization before attending law school at MU.

And youngest son, Brett, was a four-time state wrestling champion at Oak Grove and earned a wrestling scholarship to the University of Missouri, but had to give up the sport because of a health issue.

Calling the Frys a family of champions would be an understatement.

"It was competitive when the boys were growing up," Dave said. "They would see who could hit the ball the farthest, who could climb the tree the highest, and who could eat his meal the fastest."

Ryan (left) and Shaon were standouts in their respective MU careers.
Photo courtesy of the Fry Family

"It was a great atmosphere and I couldn't be prouder of the way they all turned out."

And now, the younger Frys can say the same thing about their dad.

Fry was a teacher for 28 years, a coach for 24 years, and the head baseball coach at Fort Osage for 21 years.

He has worked with some of the finest talent this area has ever produced, including St. Louis Cardinals Most Valuable Player Albert Pujols, who was an all-state infielder on his second state championship team.

"I feel blessed, as a coach and as a person, to have worked with some great young men," he said. "They loved the game as much as I do, and we were able to reach our goals together."

SHAON FRY

The only Missouri wrestler ever to win two Big 8 Conference championships and the only Tiger ever to make it to an NCAA championship match, where he placed second. His wife, Shannon, is a former MU Golden Girl who now coaches that group.

I was thrilled to be a part of the great tradition at the University of Missouri. I got to compete in the Big 8 and I was close to home so my family could come watch me compete. Looking back on it, I spent a lot of time in the gym and a lot of time hitting the books – but that's why I was there. I wasn't going to have a pity party or steal from Peter to pay Paul – I was at Missouri to get a great education and to wrestle.

The 1993 season, when I won the Big 8 Conference championship, I just got on an amazing run. I lost the NCAA championship to Ray Miller from Arizona State. The next year, I was third at the NCAA championships. I'm proud of what I accomplished and I was honored to be inducted into the Missouri Hall of Fame in 1999. Having my dad go into the Missouri Coach's Hall of Fame that same year made it even more special.

Why do the K-State cheerleaders wear bibs?

To keep the tobacco juice off their uniforms.

It was great having Ryan and Brett at Missouri. I remember being with Ryan when the doctor told him he had a blood clot in his arm and he couldn't pitch any more, and how devastated he was. But he is such a great competitor that he came back and became one of the best hitters in Missouri history. An injury ended Brett's wrestling career far too soon, but we were all proud of all of his accomplishments.

I met my wife at school and got a great education. I had the chance to go to other schools, but I picked Missouri and it's one of the best decisions I ever made.

RYAN FRY

A four-year starter at MU, Fry was named an All-America twice and a GTE Academic All-America once. In his sophomore year, he was a finalist for College Baseball's Smith Awards as the best college baseball player in America.

I always knew I wanted to go to MU because my older brother, Shaon, was there and he loved it. But after I got there, I encountered a strange turn of events. I was a pitcher in high school and was recruited as a pitcher. I went to Missouri to pitch, but my first fall at the university, I was diagnosed with a blood clot in my pitching arm. Shaon went with me to see Dr. Pat Smith, and I was so thankful he was with me. I had this thing going on with my arm and we didn't know what it was. I'd pitched a lot in high school and never had a problem. We were thinking it was a spider bite or an allergic reaction – we never even thought about a blood clot. My right arm was swollen up twice its normal size, and we later found out that it was filled with blood. They did a bunch of tests and I had no idea what was going on. I'd been a pitcher all my life, and nothing could have prepared me for the news from Dr. Smith. He came into the room and said, "Ryan, you may not be able to play ball again."

My eyes teared up. Not play ball again? I'd been playing ball all my life. Shaon told me, "Take it easy, we're going to get through this." I don't know if I could have gotten through that day without him. They put me on blood thinners and told me not to shave with a razor, for fear that I might cut myself. They told me if I got injured in a car wreck, I could bleed out before help got there – all great news for a 19-year-old kid who was ready to take on the world.

Well, to make a long story shot, I had a rib bone and collar bone that were too close, and they were closing off the flow of blood in one of my veins. But another vein started carrying the blood and it all worked out. I wasn't able to pitch again, but I could still play ball. I had a miserable year, but my sophomore year I did well (hitting .387) and I hit pretty well my junior year (.377). I went to MU to pitch and wound up having a pretty decent career as a hitter.

As I look back, it's kind of funny how it all worked out. Shaon had the chance to go to Harvard or Nebraska, and he chose MU. My first choice was Wichita State, because they were the strongest (baseball) school in the Midwest at that time. But we both decided on MU and then Brett came to MU, too. It was really pretty neat to have all three brothers at one school.

BRETT FRY

Four-time state wrestling champion at Oak Grove High School. His MU career was cut short by pancreatitis.

I was getting a lot of attention from schools after winning four state championships at Oak Grove High School. With Shaon and Ryan going to MU, it seemed like the perfect fit for me. With mom and dad both being teachers, and the fact that MU offered me a nice scholarship, it was the perfect choice for me and my family.

I didn't have near the success at Missouri that I had in high school. My sophomore year I got pancreatitis. Your pancreas secretes insulin and I don't know if I got it from weight loss or weight gain – the doctors never could really figure it out. But when I worked out or wrestled, my heart rate would go sky-high and I had a burning pain in my stomach that I couldn't handle. I have a high threshold for pain, but not that kind of pain.

I was miserable. I simply couldn't compete. The university was great and honored my scholarship and I got a great education. I have wonderful memories of MU and I loved to go down and watch Ryan and Shaon compete.

I graduated in 1995, and occasionally, I still have flare-ups with my stomach. I've just learned to live with it. It's not nearly as bad as it used to be, though.

SHANNON FRY

University of Missouri Golden Girls coach and wife of Missouri Hall of Fame wrestler Shaon Fry.

I'm pretty proud of the Fry brothers, but I'm biased because I'm married to one of them. They're a lot of fun to be around, and even though we've all been out of school for a long time, they're still competitive. I don't care what they're doing, they want to be the best. I think that's what made them such great athletes. I've talked with Shaon about him going to MU and he had a lot of other choices. For me, it was the only choice. I'm a small-town girl from Macon, Missouri, and MU was all I ever heard about or knew about. I've loved Missouri sports for as long as I can remember and I always dreamed of going to Missouri and being a part of it.

My mom had to talk me into trying out for the Golden Girls. I was shy and didn't think I had a chance of making it, but I went. I was so intimidated – and if it hadn't been for my mom, I would have never tried. I made it, and well, like they say, the rest is history. I've often wondered how my life would be different if I hadn't gone to that audition. I was a team captain and because of the Golden Girls I got to travel all over the world. We went to Tokyo; I've met presidents; national celebrities, like Magic Johnson; and for the past 11 years – this is my 12th year – I've been coaching the girls. People always ask how I met Shaon, and I can tell you it wasn't exactly love at first sight. An assistant wrestling coach worked with my brother, so I kind of knew who Shaon was. We had a psychology class together and we would talk between classes. That's how it all started – it really had nothing to do with him wrestling or me being a Golden Girl. We just met and really connected. After we graduated, we moved to Kansas City. After about three years, I was asked to come back to coach the girls. All the moons and stars and planets must have been aligned because it's all worked out beautifully. We're both doing what we love and we're still a part of Missouri.

Kelcy Vanarsdall

Kelcy is part of a great Missouri family tradition that includes her parents and her sister, Katie, who is a member of the Tigers track and field team.

Kelcy Vanarsdall was the face of Fort Osage (Missouri) High School – a 4.0 student who lettered all four years in basketball, cross country, and track.

She was involved in student government, several charities, and took part in a panel discussion on the important role religion plays in her life – which isn't an easy thing to do for most teenagers.

But then, the newest member of the University of Missouri track and field team isn't your normal teenager.

"A student-athlete like Kelcy comes along once in a lifetime, if you're lucky," girls cross country and track coach Chris Earley said.

Her parents, Dennis and Cindy Vanarsdall, attended Mizzou and her sister, Katie, is a member of the Tigers' track and field team.

She is living a dream and keeping the Vanarsdall family tradition alive in TigerTown.

Odds are it won't take this human dynamo long to achieve the same recognition she enjoyed in high school.

"Oh, I don't know about that," she said. "I'm on the track team because I work hard and I'm a good kid, but I don't compare to some of the girls on the team. They're amazing – really amazing.

"I'm not going out for cross country, just track. And I've talked to the coach about doing something like the heptathlon. I really don't know what I'm going to do, but whatever I do, I'm going to give it my best shot.

Two Jayhawks were running all over the campus yelling, jumping, hollering, and hootin'. When someone stopped them and asked them why they were so excited they said, "We just finished a jigsaw puzzle in only two months!! And it said 2-4 years!"

"No one in my family pressured me to go to MU. It was always my dream. I remember when I was a kid and we'd all get in the car and drive to MU for a football game.

"Most kids would hate being in a car an hour and 45 minutes to drive to Columbia, but I could hardly wait. Now, I'm here on campus and I might have a player in class and I can tell everyone, 'I know him; he's in the same class I'm in.'

"Football, basketball – competing on the track team – I'm going to experience it all."

She also tried out for the Mizzou choir, and admits, "It was pretty intimidating. I just went to see when I could try out and the professor was there and said, 'Why don't you just try out now?' So I did."

And did she make it?

Sure.

Was there ever any doubt?

CINDY VANARSDALL

University of Missouri Class of 1985

I was the intramural queen of basketball when I went to Missouri (laughing). I played basketball and ran track in high school, but I always dreamed of going to Mizzou and I had a great time. Now, we have the two girls at Missouri and it's a dream come true. People ask us if we pushed them to go to Missouri – and we didn't. Katie and Kelcy made their own decisions. They were excited about going and they both talked about going to Missouri when they were ready for college and now, they're there. Both of our girls are at Missouri – and we're the proudest parents in the world.

DENNIS VANARSDALL

University of Missouri Class of 1975

Is there a Vanarsdall family tradition at MU? You bet there is, and I couldn't be prouder. MU has always been a part of our family's life. I've been in education most of my life and so many times, you see kids who want to do something different from their parents. They want to break away and do their own thing, go to a different school, move out of town, things like that. But not our girls. They have always said they wanted to go to MU and now that they are there, going to Columbia on weekends is even more exciting because we get to see them.

I just hope they enjoy it as much as I did. I was on the five-year plan when I went to MU. I was a freshman varsity redshirt, but I got to travel with the team and went to Air Force and West Point. Talk about a thrill. And here is how times have changed: I was a 6-foot-1, 218-pound defensive tackle and I was the heaviest defensive player we had. Now, running backs weigh 218 pounds. My sophomore year, we played in the Fiesta Bowl at Dallas Stadium against Oregon. I had two sacks against Dan Fouts. I didn't know back then that he would be a Hall of Fame quarterback. We also played at Notre Dame. Talk about thrills. For a kid who grew up in Buckner, Missouri, that was like living a dream. All I ever did at MU was play hard and work hard. I felt like I had to work harder than the next guy to keep improving. I had a hard work ethic and both my girls have the same work ethic. I think that's why they have been so successful.

KATIE VANARSDALL

University of Missouri junior

When I was a little girl, my fondest memories are of going to MU games with my family. We'd jump in the car and get all excited because we knew we were going to Columbia to see the Tigers. Now, I go to school here and it just seems like a dream come true. Our family has a great MU tradition and now, both Kelcy and I are part of it. It's so exciting to have Kelcy here at Columbia. We can share so many things. And it's not just about sports. I want to be an elementary teacher and they have such great programs here on campus. I'm already working with kids, teaching them how to read. I get as much – even more – satisfaction from that as I do from competing on the track team or watching the football team.

When I was a little kid, it was all about having fun and watching the games and Truman the Tiger. Now, it's about so much more. I now have my own family and my Missouri family. When I made my visit to Missouri, that's what impressed me the most about the coaches and the girls on the track team. They made me feel like I was a member of their family, and I hadn't even made a commitment. And the girls who throw the shot and discus are like a special family member. Even though we compete against each other every day at practice and at meets, we're all best friends. If someone throws it farther than I do, that's great, because it's helping the team.

How do you keep a KU girl from biting her nails?

Make her wear shoes.

I'm a team player. I'm not someone who is into personal accomplishments, but when I made all-conference in the discus and my dad was down there in Texas, that was pretty special. I know he was more excited than I was, and I was pretty excited. That's the family thing I've been talking about. I have my wonderful family and then I have my Missouri family – and I love both of them so much.

CHAPTER 6

Fun Facts, Some Stats, and Cool Stuff About Notable Tigers

The fashion sense may be lacking, but the passion for the Tigers is strong!
Photo courtesy of Daniel Turner

MISSOURI COLLEGE FOOTBALL HALL OF FAMERS

Name	Pos.	Years at MU	Induction Year
Bill Roper	Coach	1909	1951
Paul Christman	QB	1938-40	1960
Don Faurot	Coach	1935-42,46-56	1961
Bob Steuber	HB	1940-42	1971
James Phelan	Coach	1920-21	1973
Ed Travis	T	1919-20	1974
Darold Jenkins	C	1940-41	1976
John Waldorf	Official	1927-29	1984
Dan Devine	Coach	1958-70	1985
Johnny Roland	HB/DB	1962, 64-65	1998

RETIRED NUMBERS

Name	Pos.	Number
Johnny Roland	HB/DB	23
Roger Wehrli	DB	23
Bob Steuber	HB	37
Darold Jenkins	C/LB	42
Paul Christman	QB	44
Kellen Winslow	TE	83

FIRST TEAM ALL-AMERICAS

Name	Pos.	Number
Ed Lindenmeyer	T	1925
Paul Christman	QB	1939
Darold Jenkins	C	1941
Bob Steuber	HB	1942
Harold Burnine	E	1955
Danny LaRose	E	1960
Ed Blaine	T	1961
Conrad Hitchler	E	1962
Johnny Roland	DB	1965
Francis Peay	OT	1965
Russ Washington	OT	1967
Roger Wehrli	DB	1968
Mike Carroll	OG	1969
Scott Anderson	C	1973
John Moseley	DB	1973
Henry Marshall	WR	1975
Morris Towns	OT	1976
Kellen Winslow	TE	1978
Bill Whitaker	DB	1980
Brad Edelman	C	1981
Jeff Gaylord	DT	1981
Conrad Goode	OT	1983
John Clay	OT	1986
Devin West	RB	1998
Rob Riti	C	1999

Missouri's Retired Numbers

No. 44 Paul Christman, QB, All-America 1939 and 1940.

Christman led the Tigers to Don Faurot's first conference championship and first bowl appearance in 1939. He played in the NFL with the Chicago Cardinals and Green Bay Packers. He was Missouri's first player chosen for induction into the National Football Foundation Hall of Fame.

No. 37 Bob Steuber, HB, All-America 1942.

Steuber starred on coach Don Faurot's Split-T offense that led the nation in rushing in 1941. He was the nation's No. 3 rusher in 1941, and No. 2 in 1942. A member of the National Football Foundation Hall of Fame, he played professionally with the Cleveland Browns, Los Angeles Dons, and Buffalo Bills.

No. 42, Darold Jenkins, C-LB, All-America 1941.

Jenkins was captain of the 1941 team, which is considered to be the best of Don Faurot's 19 Missouri teams. He is a member of the National Football Foundation Hall of Fame. Jenkins was a World War II bomber pilot who was shot down on his 27th mission and spent 17 months in a German POW camp.

No. 23, Johnny Roland, HB, All-America in 1965.

Roland rushed for 830 yards as a sophomore in 1962, but spent most of the remainder of his career as a defensive back and short-yardage runner. He is one of only eight Tigers to earn all-conference honors three times.

No. 23, Roger Wehrli, DB, All-America in 1968.

Wehrli led the nation in punt returns in 1968 and set a school record with seven pass interceptions. He still holds 10 Missouri school records. He was a perennial All-Pro performer while playing for the St. Louis Cardinals from 1969-82, and was elected to the Pro Football Hall of Fame in 2007.

No. 83, Kellen Winslow, TE, All-America in 1978.

The big tight end was the Big 8 Male Athlete of the Year in 1979. He was inducted into the Pro Football Hall of Fame in 1995. Winslow was considered the best tight end in the NFL during a nine-year career (1979-88) with the NFL's San Diego Chargers.

Don Faurot and **Dan Devine** don't need numbers – they will always be No. 1 in the hearts of Missouri fans. Faurot was the head football coach from 1935-42 and 1946-56 and director of athletics from 1935-42 and 1946-66. He was a three-sport athlete at Missouri from 1922-24. He had a record of 101-79-10 during 19 seasons as the Tigers head coach. He won three conference championships and took four teams to bowl games. He was the inventor of the Split-T formation in 1941. The Tigers led the nation in rushing that year. He is a member of the National Football Foundation Hall of Fame. The playing surface at Memorial Stadium was named in his honor in 1972.

Devine was the head football coach from 1958-70 and director of athletics from 1967-70 and 1992-94. He is Missouri's winningest football coach, with a record of 93-37-7 (.704). His Tigers were the only team in the nation, during the decade of the 1960s, to never lose more than three games. His Tigers were 4-2 in bowl games and won two conference championships. A member of the National Football Foundation Hall of Fame, Devine also coached at Arizona State, with the NFL's Green Bay Packers, and at Notre Dame, where he won a national championship in 1977.

University of Missouri
Retired Basketball Numbers

Bill Stauffer, center, No. 43

Missouri's first accomplished big man, Stauffer established the MU career rebounding record from 1950-52 that stood for 31 years until it was broken by Steve Stipanovich. The center from Maryville, Missouri, grabbed 964 rebounds and set three records that still stand – 379 rebounds in 1952, with a per-game average that year of 16.5, and a career rebound average of 13.6. He was an all-Big Seven selection in 1951 and 1952, and as a senior, was team captain and All-America. He was the first Tiger ever to have his number retired, and was chosen by the Boston Celtics in the inaugural NBA draft.

Norm Stewart, forward, No. 22

Norm Stewart is the only person in Mizzou history to be inducted into the University of Missouri Intercollegiate Athletics Hall of Fame as both a student-athlete and coach. Stewart lettered at MU in basketball and baseball in 1954-56. A two-time team captain and all-Big Seven selection in basketball, the Shelbyville, Missouri, native led MU in scoring and rebounding in 1956. His 24.1 point scoring average in 1956 ranks as the fourth-best figure in school history. Stewart's career total of 1,112 points ranks 19th at MU, with 15 of those who rank ahead of him having played for him. He was drafted by and played with the St. Louis Hawks of the NBA.

Jon Sundvold, guard, No. 20

One of only two players in Big 8 Conference history (teammate Steve Stipanovich is the other) to play on four consecutive league championship teams. Sundvold played on Missouri teams that had a cumulative record of 100-28. A guard from Blue Springs, Missouri, he twice won all-conference, all-district and all-Big 8 Tournament honors, and was an All-America in 1983. At the time of his induction, he ranked third at MU in both points (1,597) and assists (382). He was a first-round pick of the Seattle SuperSonics in the 1983 draft, and also played for the San Antonio Spurs and Miami Heat.

Willie Smith, guard, No. 30

The guard from Las Vegas created unprecedented basketball excitement during his two-year career (1974-76). He took Missouri to its first outright basketball conference championship in 46 years in 1976, and nearly got the Tigers to the NCAA Final Four. Averaging 25.3 points per game, he was the Big 8's leading scorer in 1976, and scored 43 points in a loss to Michigan in the NCAA Midwest Regional championship game. He was MU's MVP, all-Big 8, and all-district in each of his two seasons, and was an all-America as a senior. He still holds six school records and scored more points (1,387) than any two-year player in school history. Smith was drafted in the second round by the Chicago Bulls in 1976.

Doug Smith, center, No. 34

The Detroit native was just the third player in Big 8 history to score more than 2,000 points and grab more than 1,000 rebounds, joining Danny Manning and Wayman Tisdale in that elite class. He ranks second in school history in scoring (2,184 points) and first in rebounds (1,305). Smith was the Big 8 Player of the Year in 1990 and 1991, an All-America, and Big 8 Male Athlete-of-the-Year in 1991, and a two-time MVP of the Phillips 66 Big 8 Tournament. He led the Tigers to the championship in 1989 and 1991. He was the sixth player chosen in the 1991 NBA draft by the Dallas Mavericks.

Steve Stipanovich, center, No. 40

The big man played on teams that won four straight conference championships from 1979-83, and twice reached the

Sweet 16 of the NCAA Tournament. The seven-footer from St. Louis finished his career as MU's second leading scorer (1,836 points) and then all-time leading rebounder (984). He began his career winning Big 8 Newcomer of the Year honors, and ended it as the league's Player of the Year. He was the second player taken in the 1983 NBA draft and played six seasons for the Indiana Pacers.

Notable Missouri Alumni

Arts, film, and literature

- Tom Berenger (BA 1971), actor
- Kate Capshaw (BS 1975), actress
- Chris Cooper (BGS 1976), actor
- Sheryl Crow (BS Ed 1984), musician
- Matthew C. Dudenhoeffer (BS IE 1991, MPA), guitarist for rock band Gravity Kills
- Mary Stella Fernandez, now Kunze (BSIE 1990, MSIE 1992)
- Blake Green (BA 2004), interpretive dancer
- Jon Hamm, actor
- William Least Heat-Moon (BA 1961, MA 1962, PhD 1973, BJ 1978), author
- Robert Loggia (BJ 1951), actor
- Harris Merton Lyon, short story writer
- Richard Matheson (BJ 1949), author and screenwriter
- Marijane Meaker (BA 1949) novelist
- Suniti Namjoshi, writer
- Michael Patrick, (PhD 1966), author
- Brad Pitt, actor (Journalism School, but did not graduate)
- Ed Sanders (dropout 1958), poet, lead singer of the Fugs, social activist, author
- George C. Scott, actor

- Mort Walker (BA 1948), cartoonist (A life size bronze statue of his creation *Beetle Bailey* sits in front of the alumni center.)
- Tennessee Williams, playwright

Athletics

Baseball

- Phil Bradley (also played football), former MLB player
- Ian Kinsler, current All-Star MLB second baseman, Texas Rangers
- Dave Otto, former MLB player
- Jerry Schoonmaker (also played football), former MLB player
- Art Shamsky, former MLB outfielder and Israel Baseball League manager
- Mike Shannon (attended), former MLB player and current broadcaster
- Gene Stephenson (also played football), current Wichita State University baseball head coach

Basketball

- John Brown, former NBA player
- DeMarre Carroll, current NBA player for Memphis Grizzlies
- Al Eberhard, former NBA player
- Thomas Gardner, current NBA player for Atlanta Hawks
- Keyon Dooling, current NBA player for New Jersey Nets
- Linas Kleiza, former NBA player, currently with Olympiacos in the Greek League and Euroleague
- Gary Leonard, former NBA player
- Anthony Peeler, former NBA player
- Kareem Rush, current NBA player for Philadelphia Sixers
- Doug Smith, former NBA player
- Norm Stewart (BA 1956), All-America and former head coach at Northern Iowa (1961–67) and Mizzou (1967–99)
- Steve Stipanovich, former NBA player

- Jon Sundvold, former NBA player
- Jevon Crudup, former NBA player

Football
- Victor Bailey, former NFL player
- Gary Barnett 1969, former head football coach at Northwestern and Colorado.
- Dwayne Blakley, current NFL player for Tennessee Titans
- Colin Brown, current NFL player for Kansas City Chiefs
- Sam Budzyna, former NFL player
- Lloyd Carr, former head coach at University of Michigan
- Paul Christman, College Football Hall of Famer, former NFL player and broadcaster
- Brock Christopher, current NFL player for Atlanta Falcons
- Chase Coffman, All-America, John Mackey Award winner, current NFL player for Cincinnati Bengals
- Chase Daniel, All-America, current NFL player for New Orleans Saints
- Lamont Downer
- Robert Delpino, former NFL player
- Atiyyah Ellison, current NFL player for Jacksonville Jaguars
- Don Faurot, legendary MU coach and player
- Will Franklin, current NFL player for Oakland Raiders
- Justin Gage, current NFL player for Tennessee Titans
- Tony Galbreath, former NFL player
- Andy Gibler, former NFL player
- Mel Gray, former NFL player
- Ziggy Hood, current NFL player for Pittsburgh Steelers
- Harry Ice, MVP of 1942 Sugar Bowl, longtime member of athletic department
- Mike Jones, former NFL player
- Kent Layman
- Jim Leavitt, head coach at University of South Florida
- Rick Lyle, former NFL player

- Jeremy Maclin, two-time first-team All-America, current NFL player for Philadelphia Eagles
- Henry Marshall, former NFL player
- Steve Martin, former NFL player
- C.J. Mosley, current NFL Player for Cleveland Browns
- Damien Nash, former NFL player
- Brock Olivo, former NFL player
- Gus Otto, former NFL player
- Howard Richards, former NFL player
- Johnny Roland, current NFL coach and former player
- Martin Rucker, All America, John Mackey Award winner, current NFL player for Cleveland Browns
- Andy Russell, former player for Pittsburgh Steelers
- Jason Simpson
- Brad Smith, current NFL player for New York Jets
- Justin Smith, current NFL player for San Francisco 49ers
- Stryker Sulak, current NFL player for Green Bay Packers
- Roger Wehrli, 7-time Pro Bowl NFL player and member, Pro Football Hall of Fame
- James Wilder, former NFL player
- Kellen Winslow, College and Pro Hall of Fame player
- Otis Smith, former NFL player
- Russ Washington, former NFL player
- Bruce Van Dyke, former NFL player
- Eric Wright, former NFL player

Other

- Christian Cantwell, current world-class shot putter, 2004 IAAF World Indoor Champion
- Carl Edwards, current NASCAR driver
- Colleen O'Toole Gibler, former professional triathlete
- Brian Tucker, former professional soccer player, Fulham FC (England)
- Charles Cooper, three-time world Bear Wrestling champion

- Derrick Peterson, current professional runner, 2004 Olympian
- Gene Snitsky, current professional wrestler
- Evan Bourne, current professional wrestler
- Babak Torgoley, former Turkcell Super League soccer player
- Joseph Clemons, reverend, philanthropist, professional cliffhanger, and life coach

Business

- Ralph W. Babb (BS BA 1971), chairman and CEO, Comerica
- Mark E. Burkhart (BS BA 1976), president and CEO, Colliers Turley Martin Tucker
- Morris Burger (BS 1961), chairman of Burgers' Smokehouse; largest country cured ham producer in the world.
- Jack E. Bush (BS 1961), chairman of Burgers' Smokehouse; largest country cured ham producer in the world.
- Jack E. Bush (BS BA 1958), former president and director of Michaels; president of Raintree Partners
- Tom Carnahan (JD 1995), founder of Wind Capital Group, developer of wind farms
- Harry M. Cornell, Jr. (BS BA 1950), chairman Emeritus, Leggett & Platt, Inc.
- Harvey P. Eisen (BS BA 1964, ZBT, QEBH), chairman of Bedford Oak Advisors
- Alan Greenberg (BS BA 1949), chairman, Bear Stearns Companies
- David S. Haffner (BS 1974, MBA 1980), President and CEO, Leggett & Platt, Inc
- Harold S. Hook (BS BA 1953), former President, CEO, and Chairman, American General Insurance
- Edward D. "Ted" Jones (1947), managing partner of Edward Jones Investments
- R. Crosby Kemper (AB 1914), former President and Chairman, United Missouri Bancshares
- R. Crosby Kemper, Jr. (AB 1949), former President and Chairman, United Missouri Bancshares

- Richard Kinder (BA 1966. JD 1968), chairman and CEO, Kinder Morgan, and former President, Enron. With a net worth of $3.5 billion, Kinder is currently tied for No. 105 on the 2008 Forbes 400 list of richest Americans.

- E. Stanley Kroenke (BS BA 1971, MBA 1973), Chairman, THF Realty, owner, NBA's Denver Nuggets, NHL's Colorado Avalanche; co-owner NFL's St. Louis Rams, majority shareholder Arsenal FC. With a net worth of $3.5 billion, Kroenke is currently tied for No. 105 on the 2008 Forbes 400 list of richest Americans.

- Kenneth Lay (BA 1964, MA 1965), former CEO of Enron

- Harry J. Lloyd (BJ 1950), founder of House of Lloyd and the upscale Loch Lloyd village and country club near Kansas City

- Steve Lumpkin (BS BA 1977), CFO & Treasurer, Applebee's International

- Bruce B. Melchert (1961), VP of government affairs, Clarion Health, and International Founder and past Executive Director of Tau Kappa Epsilon

- James C. Morton, Jr. (JD 1972), senior VP Finance & Administration, Nissan North America

- David C. Novak (BJ 1974), chairman, CEO, and President, Yum! Brands, Inc.

- Gary L. Rainwater (BS EE 1969), CEO and President, Ameren

- Edward Rapp (BS BA 1979), vice president, Caterpillar, Inc.

- Rodger O. Riney (BS CiE 1968, MBA 1969), founder of Scottrade, deep-discount brokerage firm

- Matthew K. Rose (BS BA 1981), chairman, CEO, and President, Burlington Northern Santa Fe

- William S. Thompson, Jr. (BS CiE 1968), CEO and Managing Director of Pacific Investment Management Company (PIMCO)

- Roger M. Vasey (BS BA 1958), former Executive Vice President of Merrill Lynch & Co.

- Samuel M. Walton (BA 1940), founder of Wal-Mart

- Phillip J. Yeckel (1933), founder of Hidden Valley Ranch

Journalism

- Mike Hegedus (broadcaster) CNBC, executive producer McKinley Reserve Media Group (BJ 1971)
- John Anderson (BJ 1987), ESPN SportsCenter host
- William Springer, producer, comedian, civil rights activist, KMOX
- Douglas F. Attaway (1910-1994), publisher of defunct *Shreveport Journal* and former owner of KSLA-TV, the CBS affiliate in Shreveport, Louisiana
- Gerald M. Boyd, former Managing Editor of the *New York Times*, first African American metropolitan editor and managing editor of the New York Times
- Barney Calame, public editor, *New York Times* Company
- Jann Carl, (BJ 1982) weekend anchor/correspondent, Entertainment Tonight
- John Mack Carter, former president, Hearst Corporation
- Sophia Choi, CNN Headline News anchor
- Dennis Dodd, CBSSportsline columnist
- Kit Doyle, Southeast Missourian world-renowned photojournalist
- Clifton C. Edom (BJ 1946), Mizzou photojournalism educator and co-founder of Pictures of the Year, Missouri Photo Workshop, and Kappa Alpha Mu
- Pat Forde, ESPN columnist
- Martin Frost (BJ 1964, ZBT), political commentator, Fox News Channel
- Major Garrett (BJ 1984), national correspondent, Fox News Channel
- John Graham, chairman and CEO, Fleishman-Hillard, Inc.
- Mike Hall, the first winner of the ESPN "Dream Job" series
- Lee Hills, former chairman and CEO, Knight-Ridder Inc.
- Robert Horner (BJ 1970), president of NBC News Channel
- Juliet Huddy, FOX News host
- Walter E. Hussman, Sr. (1906-1988) owner of newspaper chain in south Arkansas, including *Arkansas Democrat-Gazette* in Little Rock, cable systems, and radio stations

- Michael Kim, ESPNEWS host
- Jim Lehrer, PBS news anchor
- Andrea Mackris, FOX News Television Producer
- Linda Marx (BJ), writer, *People Weekly*, freelance journalist, author
- Russ Mitchell (BJ 1982), anchor, CBS Evening News Sunday, CBS News
- Jonathan Murray (BJ 1977), executive producer and co-creator of MTV's Real World
- Joel Myers sports Play-By-Play Voice, Various
- Lisa Myers (BJ 1973), Senior Investigative Correspondent, NBC News
- James O'Shea, editor, *Los Angeles Times*
- Ken Paulson, editor, *USA Today*
- Chuck Roberts (BJ 1971), CNN news anchor
- Charles Griffith Ross, press secretary for President Harry S. Truman
- Brian Sandalow, *McAllen Monitor*, Texas
- Jon Scott, FOX News anchor
- Edgar Snow, main Western journalist in Mao's China
- Brian Storm (MA 1997), president/founder of MediaStorm, former vice president of Corbis
- Lee Strobel (BJ 1974), journalist and author of *The Case for Christ* series
- Joyce King Thomas (BJ 1978), Chief Creative Officer, McCann-Erickson Worldwide
- Wright Thompson, ESPN Senior Writer
- Elizabeth Vargas (BJ 1984), ABC News anchor/correspondent and 20/20 co-anchor
- Nick Wagoner (BJ 2004), Sports Writer, St. Louis Rams
- Seth Wickersham, ESPN Senior Writer
- Matt Winer (BJ 1991), ESPN SportsCenter host
- Megan Schumacher, editor with Florida Freedom Newspapers

Government and law

- Emily Newell Blair, an American writer, suffragist, national Democratic Party political leader, a founder of the League of Women Voters, and feminist.
- Russ Carnahan (BS 1979, JD 1983), U.S. Congressman
- William S. Cowherd 1881), former Democratic mayor of Kansas City, Missouri, in 1892-1893 and U.S. Congressman from Missouri in 1897-1905
- Paul Coverdell, former U.S. Senator (GA); died 2000
- William B. Cravens 1893, former U.S. Representative from Missouri
- Randy "Duke" Cunningham, former U.S. Congressman from California who resigned in 2005 amid a bribery scandal
- Gen. Donald Dawson 1932, former aide to President Truman, Curator of the Truman Presidential Library
- Martin Frost (BJ 1964) former U.S. Congressman
- Hon. John R. Gibson (BA 1949, JD 1952, TKE, QEBH), Senior Judge, U.S. Court of Appeals for the Eighth Circuit
- Sam Graves (BS 1986), U.S. Congressman
- Chuck Gross (BA 1981, MPA 1982), Missouri State Senator.
- Bob F. Griffin (JD 1958), Speaker of Missouri House of Representatives for 15 years
- Kate Hanley, nee Keith (BA 1965, BS 1965), Virginia politician
- Martin Heinrich (BS 1995), current U.S. Congressman from New Mexico
- Kenny Hulshof (BA 1980, Farmhouse), U.S. Congressman
- James P. Kem 1910,United States Senate from Missouri, 1947 to 1953
- Lloyd E. Lenard, (MS, advertising and merchandising), Caddo Parish (Louisiana) commissioner, businessman, author
- Stephen N. Limbaugh, Sr. 1951, U.S. Federal District Court Judge and former president of the Missouri Bar Association.
- Claire McCaskill (AB 1975, JD 1978), former Missouri State Auditor and current junior U.S. Senator from Missouri

- Bruce B. Melchert (1961), former Chairman, Indiana Republican Party, and former Deputy Mayor, City of Indianapolis
- Thomas L. Rubey 1885, former U.S. Representative from Missouri
- Sally Shelton-Colby, Ambassador to Grenada and Barbados from 1979 to 1981
- Ike Skelton (AB 1953, JD 1956), U.S. Congressman, Chairman of the House Armed Services Committee
- Kimbrough Stone (1895), judge of the U.S. Circuit Court of Appeals, Eighth Circuit
- Lisa White Hardwick (BS 1981) Harvard (JD 1984), Missouri Court of Appeals Judge

Governors

- James T. Blair, Jr. former Missouri Governor
- Mel Carnahan, former Missouri Governor, only person elected U.S. Senator posthumously
- John M. Dalton, former Missouri Governor
- Forrest C. Donnell, former Missouri Governor
- Warren E. Hearnes, former Missouri Governor, namesake of the Hearnes Center
- William Jayne, first Governor of Dakota Territory
- Tim Kaine, current Governor of Virginia
- Ted Kulongoski (undergraduate and law degrees), current Governor of Oregon
- Guy B. Park, former Missouri Governor
- Roger B. Wilson, former Missouri Governor

Science and technology

- Bruce Barkelew (AB 1984), creator of ProComm and co-founder of Datastorm Technologies, Inc.
- Linda Godwin (MS 1976, PhD 1980), NASA astronaut
- William T. Kane (PhD., 1966), physicist in field of fiber optics

- Richard N. Richards (BS ChE 1969), NASA astronaut
- Herschel Roman (PhD 1942), early pioneer in yeast genetics[12]
- William C. Schwartz (MA 1951), Physicist, Laser pioneer, and founder of International Laser Systems
- Larry Smarr (BA 1970, MS 1970), physicist; founding director of the National Center for Supercomputing Applications
- Thomas Smith (AB 1984), co-founder of Datastorm Technologies, Inc.
- Debbye Turner (DVM 1991), veterinarian and former Miss America
- Ernest Lenard Hall (BS EE 1965, MS 1966, PhD 1971), roboticist
- Huda Salih Mahdi Ammash (PhD 1983), WMD Scientist for Saddam Hussein, one of the 55 most wanted Iraqis post-Coalition invasion
- Brent "Mitch" Thieman (MD 2008), internal medicine physician

Authors

Bill Althaus is an award-winning columnist for *The Examiner* in eastern Jackson County, Missouri. The Simone Award Committee named him the media personality of the year in 2006 and presented him with the Gordon Docking Award. He followed that honor with the Morris Excellence in Journalism Award in 2007. The Independence, Missouri, native has also been honored by the Missouri Press Association, the Associated Press and United Press International.

Photo courtesy of
Brian Mangan

Rich Zvosec (pronounced zuh-VOH-sick) is a television basketball analyst for ESPN, a speaker, and an author. He was also a successful college basketball coach at the University of Missouri-Kansas City. Coach Z was named the Northeast Conference Coach of the Year in 1990, and the Mid-Continent Conference, the *College Insider*, and CBS Sportsline Coach of the Year in 2005.

Rich Wolfe's books have sold well over a million copies in the United States. Wolfe has authored the best-selling books in the history of Notre Dame and the Chicago Cubs. The Iowa native is the only person to appear on both *Jeopardy!* and ESPN's *Two-Minute Drill*. In 2006, he was inducted as one of Leahy's Lads at Notre Dame.